"Good Guys Don't Wear Hats"

Children's Talk About the Media

"Good Guys Don't Wear Hats"

Children's Talk About the Media

Joseph Tobin

tb

Trentham Books
Stoke on Trent
England

TEACHERS
COLLEGE
PRESS

Teachers College
Columbia University
New York and London

Published by Teachers College Press, 1234 Amsterdam Avenue, New York, NY
10027

Published in Great Britain and Europe by Trentham Books Limited

Library of Congress Cataloging-in-Publication Data

Tobin, Joseph Jay.
   "Good guys don't wear hats" : children's talk about the media / Joseph J. Tobin.
     p.cm.
   Includes bibliographical references and index.
   ISBN 0-8077-3886-7 (pbk.)—ISBN 0-8077-3887-5 (cloth)
    1. Mass media and children.   2. Children—Attitudes.   3. Children—Language.
 I. Title.
   HQ784.M3 T63   2000
   302.23′083—dc21   99-053663

ISBN 0-8077-3886-7 (paper)
ISBN 0-8077-3887-5 (cloth)
U.K. ISBN 1858561183

Printed on acid-free paper
Manufactured in the United States of America

07 06 05 04 03 02 01 00   8 7 6 5 4 3 2 1

Contents

Acknowledgments

When I began this study back in 1992, I was new to the field of media studies. Fortunately, I had some excellent guides right in my own home. Even as little boys, my sons, Sam and Isaac, were wise and knowledgeable media watchers. I learned much of what I know about children and television from hours spent watching and talking about TV and movies with my sons. Now grown, Sam and Isaac have become students not just of popular culture but also of cultural theory. Their insight into contemporary culture and cutting-edge theory has aided me in researching and writing this book. The other help with this project that I received at home came from my wife, Beth Fowkes Tobin, who is a professor of literature and a cultural studies scholar. The method I developed for this study—applying literary and poststructural theory to the analysis of children's talk—depended on my cribbing books, ideas, and perspectives from Beth. I believe that most original work occurs when a researcher in one field borrows methods and theory from another field. This is much easier to do for a professor of education who lives with a literary scholar.

I also got help with this project from outside my immediate family. As I started to read media theory, I came across the work of David Buckingham, who I quickly decided was the most creative and insightful of researchers in this field. In 1994 I sent David a fan letter, and he graciously invited me to visit him at the Institute of Education in London. Wanting more of his help, I arranged first for David, and then the next summer his colleague Julian Sefton-Green, to come to Hawai'i to teach courses in media education. Co-teaching with David and Julian was a valuable professional experience.

In 1997, the research for this book was done, and I was ready to write. I chose to go to England for my sabbatical leave to write this book so I could continue to draw on the help of David and Julian, and more generally on the sophistication of media education researchers and teachers in England—the United Kingdom is decades ahead of the United States in introducing media studies to the curriculum. During my stay in England Julian, his partner, Allyson, and their son, Sam, were gracious friends, hosts, and cultural guides.

Many people have read drafts of this book. My brothers, Lad, Jeff, and Dan, and sister-in-law Marta Savigliano all gave me helpful and supportive feedback. Dan's children, Julia and Nathan, who are the same ages and have much the same media tastes as the children I studied at Koa Elementary School, were expert informants.

Over the past 7 years, I have been in reading, writing, and research groups with an overlapping and evolving collection of colleagues and doctoral students. Simon Dentith introduced me to the writings of V. L. Voloshinov. Lois Yamauchi collaborated with me on a video pen pal project with the Hawaiian-language immersion students at Koa Elementary School, and she helped me sort out issues of local identity in Hawai'i. Since we began our jobs together in Hawai'i in 1990, Rich Johnson and I have collaborated on a wide range of ventures, including not just reading and writing groups, but also soccer playing and organizing meetings of the Reconceptualizing Research, Theory, and Practice in Early Childhood Education group. Other writing group members who gave me valuable feedback on this book include my doctoral students Donna Grace, Kerri-Ann Hewett, Gail Boldt, Julie Kaomea, and Hannah Tavares, and my faculty colleagues Mike Hayes, Chris Yano, and John Zuern.

The research at Koa was a team effort. Rich Johnson helped to conceptualize the project. Donna Grace collaborated with me on every step of the research. Andy Jacobs was instrumental in the development of the video production curriculum at Koa, and Donna took the lead on the analysis of Koa students' video productions, which become the subject of her dissertation reseach (Grace & Tobin, 1997). Lilinoe Andrews conducted the interviews in Hawaiian with the Hawaiian-language immersion students, and she analyzed this material for her master's project. Ralph Ohta collaborated with me on a project involving children's understanding of parody (Ohta & Tobin, 1995). Sarah Carmichael transcribed the tapes. The McInerey Foundation provided vital financial support.

I am grateful to Gladys Topkis for her editorial advice and encouragement at the beginning of this project. Peer reviews by Amos Hatch and Peggy Miller were very helpful in guiding my rethinking and rewriting of the manuscript. I am grateful to Susan Liddicoat for inviting me to bring this book to Teachers College Press, and to Tareth Mitch for production editing.

Finally and most importantly, I am in debt to the administrators, teachers, and especially the children at Koa Elementary School in Pearl City, Hawai'i. Thank you Lacey, Jessica, Clem, Punihei, Michael, and the other Koa kids for talking to me about movies. I'm sure the readers of this book will agree that yours are the richest and most compelling voices here.

CHAPTER 1

Introduction

What are we to make of the following comments by a group of 6-year-olds who have just been shown a scene from *Swiss Family Robinson* in which the Robinsons successfully repel an attack by a ragtag army of Asian and Polynesian pirates?

INTERVIEWER: How can you tell who are the good guys and who are the bad guys?
KEONI: 'Cause the good guys don't have, uh, hats.
KENCHIRO: 'Cause the good guys are more smarter than the bad guys.
DYLAN: The bad guys don't have horses or anything.
ELIJAH: Or a nice house.

In the action-packed scene the children are discussing here, the heroes, a well-dressed and groomed White family, demonstrate great bravery and intelligence as they use rifles, tigers, coconut bombs, and logs to repel the attack of an army of pirates, who are all people of color who dress in ragged clothes, speak in grunts, and act savagely (which is to say wildly, stupidly, impulsively, and immorally). The males in the Robinson family, including their 8-year-old son, are brave and capable fighters. The females for the most part stand behind the males, loading guns and shouting, "Look out!" The violence in the scene is continual but cartoonish, with comical special effects, no blood, and cheerful music.

Listen to a group of 7-year-old girls and boys discussing the scene:

INTERVIEWER: Who were the good guys in that movie?
NOLAN: The ones that was winning.
MARY-JEAN: The ones with the coconut bombs.
INTERVIEWER: Were there any bad guys?
DEREK: Yeah, the Indians.

INTERVIEWER: Is there a difference between the way the good guys and the
    bad guys look?
NOLAN: Yeah, because one was the Indians and one was the Americans.
INTERVIEWER: Which was the good ones?
NOLAN: The Americans.
INTERVIEWER: Did you see any girls that were with the bad guys?
DEREK: No.
INTERVIEWER: Why do you suppose that is?
NOLAN: Cuz Indians don't have girls.
MARY-JEAN: Yes, they have girls, only some.
NOLAN: Only the boy Indians fight when they go out.
INTERVIEWER: What do you suppose the girls were doing?
DEREK: Staying home.
NOLAN: Taking care of babies.

Or, finally, a group of 8-year-old girls discussing the same scene:

INTERVIEWER: Were there good guys and bad guys?
CHILDREN [in chorus]: Yes.
INTERVIEWER: Who was the good guy?
MALIA: The ones inside the house.
LOREEN: The one who was [chopping motion] . . .
INTERVIEWER: And who were the bad people?
MALIA: The ones who were outside.
LOREEN: The ones coming up.
INTERVIEWER: How can you tell who were the good ones and who were the
    bad ones?
JAYLYNN: Because they were attacking.
LACEY: No, because they look, they look . . .
INTERVIEWER: 'Cause they're attacking?
LACEY: No, because they look like, they look more bad and more good.
INTERVIEWER: What makes the bad ones look bad? I don't know what you
    mean.
LACEY: [pulling on the corners of her eyes]: Like Chinese eyes.

Clearly, a lot is going on here; there is much to be figured out. Why do
the children think good guys have horses and nice houses? Why do they refer
to the pirates in *Swiss Family Robinson* as Indians? Why don't Indians have
girls? And the question I find most interesting and disturbing: Why does
Lacey, who is Asian American (as well as Native Hawaiian), tell me that she
knows the bad guys by their "Chinese eyes"? This book is my attempt to give

some answers to these and other questions about how children think and talk about media representations of violence, gender, race, colonialism, and class.

GETTING BEYOND THE EFFECTS PARADIGM

In the last sentence, I used the phrase "think and talk about" rather than "are affected by" because I want to distance myself from the media effects paradigm. In most writing on children and media, movies and television are depicted as dangerous forces that have the power to reach out and grab children, harming them in various ways. There are several versions of media effects theory. Media researchers with a behaviorist bent tend to focus on the issue of violence and look chiefly for evidence of imitation. Psychodynamically inclined researchers generally conceptualize the effects of television and movies on children in terms of identification. Neo-Marxists, conceptualizing movies and television programs as vehicles of ideology, speak of children being subjectified or interpellated. To interpellate is to hail, as in hailing a cab. As Louis Althusser (1972) writes:

> Ideology "acts" or "functions" in such a way that it "recruits" subjects among individuals . . . or transforms individuals into subjects . . . by that very precise operation which I have called interpellation or hailing, and which can be imagined along the lines of the most commonplace everyday police (or other) hailing: "Hey, you there!" (p. 174)

Interpellation is a concept that is used sloppily in cultural studies (for critiques of the concept, see Abercrombie et. al, 1980; Barker, 1989). As a verb applied to the workings of ideology on subjects, it is used to refer to three different phenomena that too rarely get disentangled. The straightforward-seeming statement "The man hailed a cab" can mean that a man called out to a taxi driver who didn't hear him, or who heard him but chose to ignore his hail, or who responded to the hail by picking him up. Similarily, the statement "Disney's *Pocahontas* interpellates young viewers into the logic of patriarchy" can mean that the film carries a patriarchal message that targets children as its intended audience; or that children who watch the film attend to the message, but don't necessarily subscribe to it; or that children who watch the film come away more accepting of patriarchy than they were going into the theater. It is this last meaning with which we should be primarily concerned. But only a small proportion of the scholarship in cultural and media studies attempts to demonstrate that a specific media text has a demonstrable effect on particular viewers. This is tough to do because interpellation is hypothesized to operate not all at once but instead through the accrual over time of repeated experiences of being hailed by the same ideological message. A single incident of media interpellation, therefore, may have an effect on a viewer that is very subtle. But subtle should not be taken to mean undemonstrable. The workings of interpellation must be documented in specific cases or else the concept becomes nothing more than an article of faith among culture theorists and media critics.

Imitation, identification, and interpellation are very different concepts, drawn from different and even incompatible theories. And yet they share a belief in the power of media to harm children. It would be ridiculous to suggest that television and movies have no effect on children (or adults). Clearly, television programs and movies affect us or we wouldn't watch them. What is wrong with media effects research is not that it is concerned with the significance of television and movies in children's lives, but that its concern is too linear, decontextualized, adversarial, and unidirectional (Barker, 1997; Buckingham, 1996).

By *linear,* I am referring to the way the effects paradigm is stymied in the logic of single-cause, single-effect relations. Media effects studies generally set out to answer such questions as "Does watching television contribute to delinquency?" or "Does the absence of role models on television give Asian American children a negative self-image?" If we are to understand the complex ways in which children make meaning out of their television and movie watching, we need to ask less linear questions and employ more complex models of causation. We need to move beyond linear notions of causality to a more complex model that would allow for the possibility that one cause (say, a movie scene) can have different effects on different people, or different effects on the same person at different times, or no effect at all, or paradoxical effects.

By *decontextualized,* I am referring to the attempt by effects researchers to isolate the interaction of the medium and the viewer from the larger social context. In the worst (that is to say, the most artificial and least contextualized) versions of effects research, children are placed one at a time in an observation room and shown a scene from a movie; then their subsequent behaviors are observed and counted. Even in the more naturalistic media effects studies, researchers still attempt to connect a movie or television show to an outcome in a child without sufficient attention to the larger social world of meaning-making in which the child participates.

By *adverserial,* I am referring to the assumption that children are engaged in a battle for their souls with the movies and television shows they watch. The effects paradigm conceptualizes the media as something outside and potentially dangerous that children must ward off. The media are seen as powerful and malevolent, children as powerless, innocent, and vulnerable.

When it makes it into the American elementary school, media education is taught, along with sex and drug education, as a curriculum of prevention rather than appreciation. There is an illogical disjuncture in our society's attitude toward the image versus the word. The prevention model, which sees media texts as dangerous and child audiences as impressionable, is rarely applied to young children's engagement with print media. Most school libraries house many volumes of out-of-date textbooks, novels, and biographies for young readers that carry offensive ideological messages, but it's only moving images that children are warned to approach critically and resistantly.

By *unidirectional*, I am referring to the emphasis in cultural studies and media studies on texts rather than on the interaction between readers and texts (or between viewers and movies). Scholars in cultural studies typically analyze such popular cultural texts as Madonna videos (Fiske, 1989), video games (Provenzo, 1991), and Disney theme parks (Smoodin, 1994; The Project on Disney, 1995) and films (Bell, Haas, & Sells, 1995; Dorfman, 1983; Giroux, 1997). In these studies, the emphasis is on the text rather than the reader. Most work in cultural studies is based explicitly or implicitly on Stuart Hall's (1999) notion that cultural texts have preferred meanings that are difficult, though not impossible, for readers/viewers to resist. Media researchers who work in the cultural studies tradition can be divided into two camps according to how pessimistic they are about the power of texts over readers. Henry Giroux and Ariel Dorfman are among the media critics who focus on texts rather than audiences because they are pessimistic about the ability of readers and viewers to resist the dominant ideologies contained in media texts. For example, Giroux (1997) argues that animated Disney films are "teaching machines" that shape young viewers' understandings of patriarchy and racism. Dorfman (1983; Dorfman & Mattelart, 1984) sees Babar books and Disney cartoons as colonialist propaganda pieces that insidiously work their way into the impressionable minds of children and the lower classes.

The other camp of cultural studies researchers is more optimistic about the ability of child as well as adult readers of advertisements, movies, and television shows to construct resistant readings. John Fiske (1987), drawing on Michel de Certeau's (1984) theories of resistance in everyday life, argues that media texts such as Levi's commercials and Madonna videos are read creatively and resistantly by teenagers and other subcultural groups. Although Fiske is optimistic about the ability of young readers to resist the preferred meanings of cultural texts and Giroux is pessimistic, they share an approach to media studies in which the meanings of texts can be discerned by cultural critics without talking to audiences. This is not to say that Giroux and Fiske are against studying audiences, just that they rarely do so.

The alternative to text-centered approaches is reader-response studies, which focus on how readers make sense of texts (Iser, 1974; Tompkins,

1980). A ground-breaking reader-response contribution to the study of popular media is Janice Radway's *Reading the Romance: Women, Patriarchy, and Popular Literature* (1984). In the field of the moving image, the term "viewer response" generally is used in place of "reader response." Key viewer response studies include books by David Morley (1980, 1986) on British news shows, Dorothy Hobson (1982) on the uses and meanings viewers make out of a popular soap opera, and Ian Ang (1985) and Tamar Liebes and Elihu Katz (1990) on viewers' understandings of *Dallas*. Path-breaking studies of children as media viewers include Bob Hodge and David Tripp's *Children and Television* (1986), and David Buckingham's *Children's Talking Television* (1993) and *Moving Images* (1996). In these studies, the researchers typically show segments of television shows or movies to viewers and then interview them, usually in groups, to find out what meanings they make of the texts.

My study builds on this body of work. However, I believe that the field of viewer-response studies has not gone far enough in overcoming the limitations of the media effects tradition (Nightingale, 1996). For starters, the terms *reader response* and *viewer response* are unfortunate, as *response*, like *effect*, suggests a psychologized, even behaviorist understanding of media; this, happily, is not characteristic of much of the work in this field. Nomenclature aside, there are substantive problems with the viewer-response approach: it is still located in the linear reasoning of the effects tradition (one cause, one effect); the studies it yields often are insufficiently contextualized; and researchers in this tradition tend to treat the analysis of readers' responses too matter-of-factly. What's needed to overcome these problems is a hybrid approach—a viewer response study that includes an ethnographic attention to social and cultural context and the use of rigorous and imaginative interpretive strategies for making sense of the viewers' responses.

THE BEGINNINGS OF THE STUDY

I first visited Koa Elementary School in Pearl City, Hawai'i in the spring of 1991. The principal asked me to facilitate a staff meeting called to identify curricular goals. Out of this discussion came several initiatives, including an agreement to develop a video-literacy curriculum. The teachers, principal, and I eventually wrote a grant to develop a curriculum intended to promote literacy through video-production. The research component of the grant provided for me and three of my graduate students to study what the children at Koa already knew about movies and television before we pilot-tested our new curriculum. This study thus began as a sort of needs-assessment effort. The discussions of *Swiss Family Robinson* that are at the core of this book were intended originally to give us a baseline understanding of what the students at Koa already knew about media representations of violence, race, and gender. It was only after completing the first round of focus group interviews in 1992 that I came to appreciate the richness of the children's discussions and to see how difficult it would be to reduce them to a needs assessment.

Between the fall of 1992, when we conducted the first round of interviews, and the spring of 1997, when I wrote the first draft of this book, I spent approximately two days a week at Koa. At first, I worked alongside the teachers and children on video-production activities (see Ohta & Tobin, 1995, and Grace & Tobin, 1997, for descriptions of our video production efforts). Eventually, as the teachers, administrators, children, and I grew comfortable with one another, we entered into a "school–university partnership," and I became the coordinator of Koa's field-based teacher education program. In this role, I visited my student teachers in Koa classrooms several times a week, met regularly with the teachers, and did some demonstration teaching with the children. In 1995, I began doing some work with the children enrolled in Kula Kaiapuni, the Hawaiian-language immersion program at Koa. Over my years at the school, I came to know the Koa community very well. Like many anthropologists, I find that by the time I write my ethnography I am no longer completely an outsider looking in. And yet in another sense, as an adult, like Koa's administrators, teachers, and parents, no matter how much time I spend there, I remain an outsider to the culture of the children.

THE RESEARCH DESIGN

Because this study is centered on the analysis of children's talk about movies, I needed a research method that would produce rich conversations. As in my study of preschools (Tobin, Wu, & Davidson, 1989), I chose to use videotape to stimulate a multivocal conversation. My team and I showed groups of 6- to 12-year-old children clips from two television commercials and two movies and asked them to talk about the meaning of what they saw. We interviewed the children in groups of four to six rather than individually, on the assumption that children form their beliefs and ideas about the media through conversations with peers and with adults. To see how gender affects children's talk about popular media, we varied the gender composition of the focus groups: One-quarter of the groups were all boys, one-quarter all girls, and one-half mixed. We showed the same video clips and asked the same follow-up questions to 32 groups of children in order to produce the sense of a conversation across the groups. The 32 focus groups did not interact directly, but the 162 students who participated in the study come into dialogue with each other in the pages of this book, as we hear them discussing the same films, answering the same questions, and debating the same issues.

The procedure we used was to have each group sit around a table in the library with us for 30 minutes or so while we showed them video clips on a monitor set up at the end of the table and then asked them questions about what they had just seen. Members of our research team (Donna Grace, Christina Kimura, Lilinoe Andrews and I) took turns as interviewer. The gender and race of the interviewer undoubtedly played some part in the shape of the focus group discussions, but I have not been able to pinpoint specific effects. It doesn't seem to be the case, for example, that the girls spoke more or more openly in groups where there was a female facilitator than in the groups I facilitated, or that the Japanese American children were more honest or direct in the groups facilitated by Christina Kimura than the groups facilitated by one of the *haole* (White) members of our team.

The children were videotaped while they watched the clips and during the discussions that followed. We repeated the focus group discussions the following spring to see how the children's critical viewing skills had developed after a year of video production work. We then made transcriptions of the focus group discussions. This process yielded approximately 12 hours of videotape, which translates into 400 pages of transcript, or about 5,000 separate comments.

The video clips I used to initiate and give structure to the conversations were two commercials—one for the Teenage Mutant Ninja Turtle's Bubble Bomber, the other for Cheerios—and scenes from two movies—*Swiss Family Robinson* (1960) and *The Black Stallion* (1979). I intended to use the commercials to get the children talking about their understanding of advertising, the artfully filmed *The Black Stallion* to get at their understanding of film aesthetics and production techniques, and *Swiss Family Robinson* to get at how children make sense of the sexism, racism, and violence that can be found in many movies and TV shows made for children. However, the discussions of *Swiss Family Robinson* turned out to be so rich and complex that I decided to make the focus of this book the children's talk about this one film.

I should explain a bit about how and why I came to choose the *Swiss Family Robinson* segment. I first considered using as a stimulus tape a contemporary Saturday morning television show or a recently released movie. I eventually concluded that my study would be less quickly dated if I instead used a classic children's film that would remain in circulation for many years. For a couple of weeks in April 1992, as I was working out the plan for this study, I perused the children's section at my local video rental store looking for popular movies with scenes containing enough violence, sexism, and racism to get children talking about how they make sense of these issues in the popular media but mild enough to show to children in the context of a public elementary school. Eventually, I came upon *Swiss Family Robinson*, a movie that had been a favorite of mine when I was a child. As I watched the film for the first time in over 30 years, I found the scene that struck me as perfect for this study. Originally, I thought I would need separate clips to get at the problems of violence, sexism, and racism. But the scene where the pirates attack the Robinsons presents all three—with colonialism (and, as we shall see in Chapter 4, environmentalism) thrown in for good measure.

I learned in the course of the interviews that about half the students at Koa had previously seen *Swiss Family Robinson*, either on a rented videotape or broadcast on the Disney Channel. Many of the children also knew the outlines of the story from visiting the Swiss Family Robinson treehouse at Disneyland. A few of the children told me they had seen other versions of the movie (*Swiss Family Robinson* was first filmed in 1940, starring Freddie Bartholomew; Irwin Allen remade the film in 1975; *Mountain Family Robinson* was released in 1979; *Beverly Hills Family Robinson* was a 1997 made-for-television movie; *The New Swiss Family Robinson* was broadcast on *The Wonderful World of Disney* in 1999). The 1960 version from which I took the clip was particularly appropriate for my study at Koa, as the setting is a tropical island that looks quite a bit like Hawai'i (the movie was filmed in the Caribbean), and the ethnic composition of the actors in the movie approximates the ethnic diversity of the school and more generally of the state.

THE LOCAL SETTING

Koa is located in a neighborhood of modest single-family homes and townhouses overlooking Pearl Harbor. The children at Koa come from a mix of working-class and middle-class families. Recently, the neighborhood has grown poorer. In the slumping local economy, with real estate prices dropping, homes that were once owner-occupied have been turned into rentals. When I did the research, about 25% of the children at Koa qualified for the school lunch program. The school, like the state of Hawai'i, is racially and culturally heterogeneous. When I did the study, Koa was approximately one-quarter Native Hawaiians, one-quarter third- and fourth-generation Japanese, Chinese, and Korean Americans (on at least one side); and one-quarter more recent immigrants from the Philippines and American Samoa. There were a handful of White and African American students, most from military families. Defining the Koa student body along ethnic lines is tricky, as the most common ethnic/racial type at Koa, as in the State of Hawai'i, is "mixed." Hawaiian-born and -raised children, including most of the children at Koa, tend to refer to themselves as "locals."

Most of the children at Koa understand pidgin (technically, "Hawaiian Creole English"; see Tamura, 1994). Some also speak it, more freely on the playground than in the classroom. The transcripts I analyze are sprinkled with pidgin phrases and rhythms. What may sound like grammatical errors are, in some cases, appropriate pidgin constructions. Readers unfamiliar with pidgin will have little trouble understanding the children's speech; in the focus group discussions the Koa students used mostly standard English because the discussions were held in school and because they were being interviewed by adults (two of whom were *haoles*), whom they assumed wouldn't understand or approve of pidgin.

When I was conducting this research, Koa was home to two schools-within-a-school, one in which the language of instruction was English, the other a *Kula Kaiapuni* (Hawaiian language immersion) site in which the children were taught almost entirely in Hawaiian (Slaughter, 1997; Yamauchi, Ceppi, & Lau-Smith, 1999). In September 1992, our team held focus group discussions with the 122 first- through sixth-grade students in the English-speaking program. We later repeated this process, with the interviews conducted in Hawaiian with 40 third- and fourth-grade students enrolled in the Hawaiian-language immersion program.

This study is based on the responses of 162 children in one school, in one community, at one point in time, talking about one set of short video clips. Yet even with all these variables limited, the task of analysis is daunting—it is all I can do to make sense of what the children said in this one specific context, a locality I know very well. Koa Elementary School is one small community with a unique mix of people, language, micro-politics, and in-jokes. But this fact does not limit the significance of the story I tell here, for the world is made up of thousands, even millions, of such localities, interpretive micro-communities in which the global media culture is understood, embraced, resisted, and infused with meanings.

THE POLITICS OF RESEARCH

In research situations, children can either resist or facilitate our attempts to know them. Some of their resistance is intentional—after all, there is much at stake here. If a media researcher asks a child, "After you watch action movies, are you likely to go out on the playground and fight?," even if the child believes that the true answer to this question is "Probably," he has reason not to admit this to an adult. A tactic children used in this situation was to respond to my questions in the singsong register children reserve for answering teachers (and researchers) insincerely: "Is it bad to fight on the playground?" "Yes, Mr. Tobin." "If you watch a violent movie, will you be violent?" "No, Mr. Tobin."

The sociologist de Certeau (1984) makes a useful distinction between *strategies* (of the powerful) and *tactics* (of the weak). Teachers have strategies for educating and managing students; students have tactics they employ to resist their teachers' agendas. We researchers have strategies (research designs) for figuring out what is going on in our informants' heads; informants have tactics they can use to resist our knowing them. As I demonstrate in Chapter 2, some of the moments of resistance I encountered in this study were clearly tactical maneuvers children used to protect their access to movies with objectionable content. In some cases, the children's resistance to my project took the form of parody and play. In addition to blocking me from seeing inside them, children took pleasure in wielding power over me, as they reveled in a fact we both knew to be true: they had information I needed and which they had the power either to withhold or to produce. It therefore is unclear who was the more powerful figure, setting the rules of the game, and who was the weaker figure, reduced to tactical maneuvers. As the adult and the researcher, I had the power advantage. But it often felt to me as though it was the children who found the grounds of our conversation more familiar and who were more in control of the outcome and I who was forced to adapt and change tactics.

LOOKING AWRY AT CHILDREN'S MEDIA WATCHING

The children at Koa also resisted my desire to know how media affect them, not by intentionally teasing or tricking me, but by saying things I did not understand. In this book you will find children saying things that are stranger and less coherent than the quotes you will find in the work of other media researchers. This is in part a result of the criteria I employed as I selected key passages to analyze for each chapter. The incomprehensible statements made by child informants that end up on the cutting room floor in other researchers' studies are precisely the statements I seize on and foreground in my research. My work is also unlike that of most other viewer-response researchers in seeing the analysis of readers' responses as problematic, requiring rigorous and imaginative tools of textual interpretation. If, as recent literary theory teaches us, the meaning of a literary text is indeterminate and there is no simple or unproblematic way to make sense of the meaning of a novel or poem, surely this is also the case for interview transcripts of children talking about movies.

I don't mean to suggest that other viewer-response researchers have been sloppy or simplistic in their approach to analyzing viewer responses, but rather that the field thus far has failed to adequately problematize the task of analyzing responses or to employ sufficiently sophisticated methods of textual interpretation to make sense of the transcripts generated by their interviews and questionnaires. David Buckingham (1993, 1996) is in the forefront of the viewer-response critics who go well beyond surface meanings in their analyses of interviewer responses, as he considers factors such as the social desirability of responses in a focus group setting and the pleasure children find in fooling an adult researcher. Such considerations are a start in the right direction, but they fall short of bringing a rigorous interpretive apparatus to the analysis of viewer responses. To introduce new modes of analysis to the field of viewer-response studies, I use a variety of interpretive techniques borrowed from literary studies, psychoanalysis, performance studies, critical theory, and ethnography.

Ethnography can provide a sense of social and cultural context that is lacking in most viewer response studies (Gillespie, 1995). My study is an ethnography in that it is based on a long period of participant observation in a field setting; I treat the children as informants rather than as research subjects; I view the children's world at Koa as a community of meaning; and I understand my role to be that of an outsider attempting to describe and explain an insider's culture to other outsiders. On the other hand, the study is not an ethnography in the traditional sense because it is focused on children's understanding of media representations; it is quasi-experimental, employing structured focus group discussions based on a video cue to produce transcripts; and Koa Elementary School is not a self-contained culture but rather one local site in a complex larger society. School, classroom, and playground ethnographies are always, necessarily, ethnographies only by analogy, as these sites are not cultures in the strict sense of the term. Children's social spaces are culture-like entities located in larger real cultures, which include adults. Notably, the voices and perspectives of adult members of the Koa culture (parents, teachers, and administrators) are missing here. Or, rather, they are present but only indirectly, as they are cited, mimicked, and parodied by the children.

From anthropology, psychoanalysis, and literary theory I have taken the idea of analyzing moments in the flow of my informants' talk that reveal slippages or doublings of meanings. In *The Raw and the Cooked* (1996), Claude Lévi-Strauss demonstrates how the beliefs and values of a culture can be elucidated through the identification of core binaries. Following Levi-Strauss, I analyze the interview transcripts looking for the binaries the Koa children use to make sense of their world.

In *The Psychopathology of Everyday Life* (1901/1974), Freud shows how parapraxes ("Freudian slips") can give us insight into the workings of the unconscious. But unlike Freud, who used slips to uncover individual, intrapsychic tensions, V. N. Voloshinov (who may have been Mikhail Bakhtin writing under the name of Voloshinov—see Chapter 2) suggests that we read slips and other "double-voiced" speech acts as windows onto the conflicts and tensions of the larger society to which the speaker belongs. Slips are double-voiced because they are a combination of what Voloshinov describes as "two axiological horizons." For Freud, these differing horizons are conflicting parts of the psyche; for Voloshinov (1927/1976b), they are conflicting ideological positions and material interests in the larger society. Thus, where Freud would likely read Lacey's comment that the bad guy in the movie has "Chinese eyes" as a symptom of an identity conflict and an unconscious expression of ambivalence about being Asian American, Voloshinov would read it as a local manifestation of the conflictual and incommensurable discourses on race and ethnicity that exist in the larger American society. While I do not deny the importance of individual experience, for an understanding of such inherently socially constructed issues as media representations of race, class, gender, and violence, I find Voloshinov's sociologically inflected take on double-voicedness more useful than Freud's intrapsychic mode of interpretation. In social contexts such as discussions with a group of children at school, where we have no direct access to the psyches of the speakers, we would do well to treat speakers' words as social texts and to avoid the temptation to psychoanalyze. Or rather, as Voloshinov suggests, such situations call for a different kind of psychoanalysis, a psychoanalysis not of individual psyches and intentions, but instead of the anxieties, concerns, and tensions of the larger society as verbalized in the utterances of individuals.

In *Looking Awry: An Introduction to Jacques Lacan Through Popular Culture,* Slavoj Zizek (1991) points out the similarity between the detective and the psychoanalyst. Both professions require an ability to hone in on the critical clue, something that is:

> "odd"—"queer"—"wrong"—"strange"—"fishy"—"rummy"—"doesn't make sense," not to mention stronger expressions like "eerie," "unreal," "unbelievable," up to the categorical "impossible." What we have here is a detail that in itself is usually quite insignificant . . . but which nonetheless . . . denatures the scene of the crime and produces an . . . effect of estrangement—like the alteration of a small detail in a well-known picture that all of a sudden renders the whole picture strange and uncanny. Such clues can of course be detected only if we put in parentheses the scene's totality of meaning and focus our attention on details. Holmes' advice to Watson not to mind the basic impressions but to take into consideration details echoes Freud's assertion that psychoanalysis employs interpretation en detail and not en masse. (p. 53)

To look awry at a section of interview transcript, I begin by locating key clues or symptoms, or what deconstructionist literary critics call *aporia,* sites of doubt or perplexity where the apparent coherence of a text can be unraveled. Examples of aporia in the children's comments presented at the beginning of this chapter include Keoni's statement "'Cause the good guys don't have, uh, hats," Dylan's "The bad guys don't have horses or anything," and Elijah's "Or a nice house." These are the slightly odd but unspectacular sorts of comments that even a skilled textual interpreter at first might overlook. But the more we think about these comments, the stranger they become. If we play with them long enough, if we tug on them, we can make the surface coherence of the text unravel and thereby give us a way inside. In Chapter 6, I use these comments about hats, horses, and houses as clues to a world of values and meanings based on a dichotomy of good guys, who have families, nice clothes, nice homes, and domesticated animals and bad guys, who are nomadic, hat-wearing, shirtless men who don't have women, children, or animals, and want what is not theirs.

Another way to look awry and afresh at children's talk is to view it from the perspective of performance theory. Following Peggy Phelan's definition of performance as "representation without reproduction" (1993), we can read Lacey's "Chinese eyes" words and gesture as a performance that re-presents the racism of the Disney film without necessarily reproducing it. In three words and a gesture, Lacey has represented the semiotics of evil in *Swiss Family Robinson*—but whether her experience of watching the film has led her to internalize the film's racial message cannot be discerned through her performance alone. In Chapter 3, I use Judith Butler's notion that gender is something one performs rather than something one is or has in order to make sense of a transcript in which a group of 8- and 9-year-old boys and girls stake out gendered positions on violence and sentimentality in movies. Following Butler (1990, 1993), I view gender—and, by extension, race and ethnicity—as awkwardly written social scripts that people, once they are cast in a part, perform with as much enthusiasm and conviction as they can muster, but never totally convincingly. While Butler suggests that we view gender as performance, she warns us against seeing the performance of gender as a playful masquerade, a costume that can be put on and taken off at whim and without consequences. We perform gender, but gender categories precede our performance, and the costs of performing normative gender roles badly, or of performing deviant gender roles well, are high. The stakes also are high for performing race, ethnicity, and class. In many of the focus group discussions, I interpret what the children say as attempts to perform convincing versions of gender, ethnicity, and "localness" for themselves, for their classmates, and for me.

Looking awry at my transcripts allows me to make sense of children's talk that at first seems illogical or even incomprehensible. But this is not to suggest that once one is armed with these powerful interpretive techniques, all children's talk becomes accessible and coherent. Of the thousands of lines of text I collected of children talking about *Swiss Family Robinson*, for each of the odd or cryptic comments I have been able to interpret there is another comment that continues to elude my understanding. And even where I have been able to come up with what I feel are reasonable interpretations, I am never completely convinced that these interpretations are right.

Once again, I find Bakhtin helpful. Instead of asking if my interpretations are right or true, a Bakhtinian perspective would suggest that it is more useful to ask if they are reasonable and appropriate replies to my informants' statements. For Bakhtin, the highest ethical responsibility, not just of researchers but of human beings, is to answer the utterances of others (1990). To answer, we must first interpret what the other person is saying to us. Our answers can never be perfect because our interpretations can never be completely true—there is always, necessarily, slippage of meaning. But this slippage need not, should not, keep us from trying to make sense of and connect with others. We listen to each other, try to understand, and answer as best we can. Inevitably, we project our perspectives and preoccupations onto the words of others, and yet generally, in our interactions with fellow adults, we manage to understand each other well enough to feel that our conversations make sense. In contrast, much of what children say to us, about television and movies, about violence, race, class, gender, and other topics, doesn't make much sense to us. I suspect that most of us adults who interact with children as teachers, researchers, and parents feel bad about this—about the fact that we often give children less than our complete attention when they talk; that we listen to them, at times, without confidence that we will understand them; and that our answers to what they say to us (when we do answer) are often tinged with condescension, irritation, or befuddlement. This book is an attempt to introduce innovative modes of interpretation that increase our chances of finding sense in what children say to us and, in doing so, give us new possibilities for answering children's talk about popular media and other topics.

CHAPTER 2

Imitative Violence

The most contentious of media issues is the hypothesized effects that watching media violence has on young people, particularly on preadolescent and adolescent boys. This is the core of our society's media anxiety: the belief that watching violent movies will make impressionable young men do violent things. But how can we know whether watching representations of violence is a significant cause of violent behavior?

The popular press periodically carries stories of children and adolescents who committed crimes purportedly as a direct result of something they saw in the movies or on television. But as David Buckingham (1996) writes in an insightful analysis of one of these sensational stories (the Jamie Bulger murder), stories of media-caused violence nearly always turn out to be less than what they seem:

> Individuals who are already disposed towards violence may well take cues for their behavior from television, albeit among many other sources—yet the evidence that such sources do more than provide suggestions for the *form* of their violent behavior is very limited indeed. (p. 5)

Correlational arguments are often used to link rising rates of juvenile crime to increased hours of television watching. But correlational evidence does not prove causation. Rates of television watching, screen violence, and delinquency have all increased in the United States in the past 20 years, but so have the number of shopping malls, the popularity of frequent flyer programs, and the uses of Spandex. And if media watching causes delinquency in any simple way, how can we explain why juvenile crime rates in Canada and Japan are much lower than in the United States, even though Canadian children watch more or less the same shows as Americans do and Japanese programming is, if anything, even more violent? *The Mighty Morphin Power Rangers,* it should not be forgotten, is an import from Japan.

Some media researchers employ experimental approaches to demonstrate the workings of imitative violence. These researchers typically show children

16

violent movies in laboratory settings and then monitor their reactions, usually by leaving them alone in a room with a Bobo (punching bag) doll and watching through a one-way mirror to see what happens. Critics point out that these experiments "measure artificial responses to artificial stimuli in artificial situations" (Buckingham, 1993, p. 11). What would we expect a child to do with a punch doll other than punch it? Under these conditions, even Gandhi might have been tempted to throw a few jabs.

As an alternative to anecdotal, correlational, and experimental studies of the effects of screen violence on children, some researchers talk to children about their television and movie viewing. Bob Hodge and David Tripp introduced this line of research in 1986 with the publication of *Children and Television: A Semiotic Approach*. This work has been carried forward most effectively by Buckingham in his books *Children Talking Television* (1993) and *Moving Images: Understanding Children's Emotional Approaches to Television* (1996). As Buckingham argues, the only way we are going to find answers to our questions about young people and popular media is "by listening to the voices of children themselves, and by taking seriously what they have to say" (1996, p. 16). This is precisely my agenda in this book.

A CONVERSATION ABOUT IMITATIVE VIOLENCE

The 3-minute scene I showed the children from *Swiss Family Robinson* is loaded with cartoonish violence. There are lots of explosions and flying bodies, but no blood and no one visibly wounded or killed. After showing the clip, I asked several questions intended to open up a conversation on imitative violence. Of the 32 groups of children we interviewed, one conversation on this topic stands out as the most interesting but also most problematic—the comments of two boys, Dan and Beau, and two girls, Jordan and Stacy, ages 11 and 12:

INTERVIEWER: Some people don't like this movie. Any guesses why?
DAN: They probably think it's just dumb.
BEAU: 'Cause the world don't live like that.
JORDAN: Violence.
DAN: We know it's fiction. It's only a movie.
INTERVIEWER: Do you think this is a good movie to show kids?
BEAU AND STACY: Yeah.
DAN: No, 'cause they might go out on the streets and try to act like that. Use baseball bats like logs.
INTERVIEWER: Do you think that if you saw a movie like this it might make you more violent?

BEAU: Yeah.

DAN: Yeah, like let's do that, "Get the gun—boom."

BEAU: Shoot your friend! Ooh, ambulance.

INTERVIEWER: Do you do violent things after seeing a violent movie?

BEAU: Yeah, like a karate movie.

INTERVIEWER: That makes it sound like we shouldn't let you see movies like this. Is it bad that I showed it to you this morning?

DAN: No. It's funny. We just laughed.

INTERVIEWER: When you go to recess, are you going to throw rocks?

DAN: No. We don't have rocks out there.

STACY: We don't have coconuts.

BEAU: We just get the soccer ball, throw it at each other.

JORDAN: We know it's just a movie.

INTERVIEWER: `I'm not sure what you are saying—that you know it's just a movie or that if you watch it, it makes you more violent?

DAN: Like before you do something, before a game you see a movie or you listen to a kind of song, and it gets you all hyped up. . . .

INTERVIEWER: Should we worry about that?

DAN: No.

INTERVIEWER: If you were a parent, would you let your kids watch movies like this?

BEAU: Yeah. This is fun.

DAN: It's not *Mad Max*.

As Buckingham suggests, if we want to understand how the experience of watching media violence affects young viewers, we need to talk to them. However, as this transcript demonstrates, talking to children about their media-watching often fails to yield simple or straightforward answers to our questions. In this conversation, the students offer a series of contradictory statements about imitative violence. Within a two-minute segment of the interview, they tell me that watching violent movies both does and does not affect them.

When confronted with such inconsistencies in analyzing an interview transcript, a commonsense approach would be to see one of the two positions articulated as genuine (as revealing how the speakers really feel) and the other as untrue, something they said in order to achieve some political, social, or emotional need. Following this logic, we might hypothesize that when the students tell me that violent movie scenes lead them to act violently on the playground, this is the truth. When I follow up by saying, "That makes it sound like we shouldn't let you see movies like this," they realize there is a potential cost to having been so honest with an adult researcher and attempt to cover up by telling me, "We know it's just a movie." An equally plausible reading of this transcript would be that the students were telling the truth when they said that movies like this don't affect their behavior—they are nonviolent kids who know the difference between fictional representation and reality—and that their talk about bashing people with baseball bats and shooting their friends was just a way of acting tough and cool in front of their peers by playing the part of the hair-trigger male, easily aroused by and into violence. They also may have been getting some fun out of misleading and confusing a nosey and perhaps naive media researcher.

The inconsistencies in this transcript can be resolved in other ways as well. One would be to suggest that some of the students are susceptible to media effects and others are not, and that the contradictory statements made in the focus group interview reflect intragroup differences among the children. This explanation is reasonable but not applicable here, as several of the most directly contradictory statements are made by the same two children (Dan and Beau). Another reasonable explanation would be that Dan and Beau are confused or ambivalent. This reading would be consistent with the psychoanalytic position that contradictory statements reflect intrapsychic conflicts.

A BAKHTINIAN APPROACH

I question the assumption that the things children say about media are understood most usefully in terms of the psychological functioning of individuals. Most researchers assume that children's statements are a sort of window into what is going on inside their heads. What is the alternative? We can think of children's talk about movies as not just an expression of their preexisting thoughts and feelings, but also as positions that are being tried out and developed in the course of talking about them. And we can view children's talk about the media as expressions less of their individual concerns and understandings than of larger social concerns and understandings that get articulated by and through individuals as they speak. This is the position staked out by Bakhtin and his circle.

The confusion that surrounds the relationship of Bakhtin to his circle makes the task of citing Bakthinian ideas a bit tricky. Recent scholarship suggests that some works published under the name of V. N. Voloshinov were written entirely or in part by Mikhail Bakhtin (Clark & Holquist, 1984; Dentith, 1995; Todorov, 1984). My position is that while it seems clear that Bakhtin should be given some credit for ideas published under the name of Voloshinov, it is not clear that the right thing to do is to replace Voloshinov's name with Bakhtin's on the publications whose authorship is in question. Therefore, when referring specifically to "Discourse in Life and Discourse in Art" (1926/1976a) and to *Freudianism: A Marxist Critique* (1927/1976b), which were published within Bakhtin's lifetime, with Bakhtin's consent, under the name of Voloshinov, I cite Voloshinov. I use the adjective *Bakhtinian* to refer more generally to perspectives expressed in works published under the names of Bakhtin and his circle.

Before getting back to the question of imitative violence and to the transcript at hand, I need to introduce the four key Bakhtinian principles I will be employing in this chapter and elsewhere in this book.

The meaning of an utterance is always contextual. Things are said in certain contexts to particular people with whom the speaker shares, to a greater or lesser extent, language, assumptions, and a point of view. To understand the meaning of statements made in a focus group discussion, we therefore need to know as much as possible about the context. Voloshinov (1926/1976a) suggests that context includes the setting of the conversation; the identities of the speakers (beginning, but not ending, with each speaker's age, culture, race, class, and gender); the external texts and experiences the speakers cite, hoping that their listeners will catch their references and make appropriate associations; and what can be implied but needs not be said aloud by a community of speakers, because it is already collectively assumed to be true (an enthymeme—a part of an argument that is assumed but not expressed).

The word is only half ours. By this, Bakhtin means that we can only speak by using words, phrases, and ideas that others have used before. Utterances are composed of the citation, plagiarism, mimicry, and repetition of the voices of others. Because meaning is contextual, when we repeat someone else's words in a new context, the meaning becomes new. Because each speaker has been exposed to a unique combination of already existing words, phrases, and ideas, no two people speak in exactly the same way. Speech is creative and original because although we necessarily must cite the words and ideas of others, we continuously cobble them together in new and unique ways. Because all speech carries echoes of the voices of others, language is inherently citational, hybridized, and double-voiced.

I can best demonstrate this concept with an example from the comments of a student in another of the focus groups. Michael, who comes from a middle-class family with an at-home mother and a father who is an officer in the military, was one of several older students I interviewed who complained that adults underestimate their ability to resist media effects:

My mom says, "Michael, you know I don't like you watching that kind of movie." Or, "Michael, you know I don't like that kind of toy—it's too violent." My mom's afraid I'm going to be a mercenary, hiding in jungles and killing people, when I grow up.

Michael's use of citation is similar to the literary techniques Bakhtin discusses in *Discourse in the Novel* (1981), where he shows how novelists such as Dostoevsky and Dickens use "two-voiced discourse" to represent within a single sentence the perspectives of two or more people. A novelist, for instance, can use direct quotation (dialogue) to represent the voice of a character with whom neither the narrator nor the protagonist shares a point of view. Michael does this in the first sentence of the passage when he quotes his mother in a way suggesting that she is wrong. Because he is speaking rather than writing, Michael has the advantage over the novelist of being able to use tone of voice to emphasize his mother's ridiculousness. He not only cites his mother here, he impersonates her, using a voice (that of a biddy) that works to parody her position.

A speaker or writer can also represent the voice of another by quoting him indirectly. Bakhtin (1981) labels this technique "hybridity":

> We call hybrid construction any utterance that belongs, by its grammatical (syntactic) and compositional features, to a single speaker, but that actually contains intermingled within it two utterances, two manners of speaking, two styles, two "languages," two semantic and axiological horizons. (p. 304)

This is what Michael does in the last sentence of his statement, where, without quite quoting her, he represents his mother's position and at the same time distances himself from it: she believes that his interest in war toys as a small boy and in violent movies now has pointed him down the path to being a violent adult. He believes that her concern is ridiculous. He simultaneously presents her position and ridicules it by using indirect quotation: We can hear in his voice a caricature of her voice, saying not merely that she is concerned about Michael's exposure to violence but that she can already picture him 10 years from now killing people for money in a far off jungle. We can't be sure whether Michael is inventing this hyperbolic language in order to parody his mother, who no doubt expresses concern, but perhaps less dramatically, or if his mother uses such language ironically, to poke fun at her overprotective concern for her son.

The content of psychic life is thoroughly ideological. By this, Voloshinov means that what appear to be the neurotic concerns and confusions of individuals are more usefully conceptualized as larger social tensions, problems, and inconsistencies that are felt and expressed at the level of the individual feeling and speaking subject. In *Freudianism: A Marxist Critique* (1927/1976b), Voloshinov argues that confusion, contradiction, and stress inevitably will be felt and expressed by individuals who live in a society that is stratified, conflictual, heteroglossic, and changing (which means, in every society!).

We have an ethical imperative to answer. We can never know exactly, precisely, confidently what another person is feeling or thinking from what he or she says. The best we can do is to listen empathetically, think about what he has said to us, and then answer. In conversation, we answer as best we can, even if we don't entirely catch the meaning of the words another person says to us. We can say, "Sorry, I don't understand" just so many times in a conversation before it breaks down. After using up our quota of "Say that agains," "Pardons," and "What do you means?," we have to make a guess about the meaning of what we are hearing and answer as best we can. This is the nature not just of talking to strangers with thick accents and odd vocabularies but of all conversation, including the research interview, where a Bakhtinian ethic would demand that we not just analyze, categorize, and evaluate what our informants say but also, most importantly, answer them in some way.

How can Bakhtinian principles inform our reading of this discussion of imitative violence? In this transcript we find a group of students articulating contradictory popular positions on media effects. Bakhtin would suggest that the fact that the students say contradictory things about imitative violence does not necessarily mean that they were attempting to mislead me or that they are internally conflicted or confused. It is more useful to think of this particular conversation and, more generally, of children's talk about movies and television as local manifestations of a larger social discourse. Given our society's intellectual confusion, ideological divisiveness, and hypocrisy about media effects, why would we expect what children say on this topic to be otherwise?

ANSWERING QUESTIONS WITH CITATIONS

The Bakhtinian perspective on conversation as citation suggests a promising technique for textual analysis. We can attempt to trace the sources that are being cited—and, in some cases, mimicked or caricatured—by the students in the transcript. In the transcript, we find students citing various common ideological positions from the larger social discourse on young men's susceptibility to media representations of violence. It is as if these children are contestants in a game show whose rules require that every question be answered with something people commonly say about children and the media.

Effect on Youth Crime

"They might go out on the streets and try to act like that" and "Get the gun—boom" can be read as citations/caricatures of the most panicky of our society's media fears. "They might go out on the streets" is an odd thing for an 11-year-old to say about the effect a movie set on a tropical island might have on his contemporaries. But the remark begins to make sense when we consider how the word "street" functions in the public discourse about imitative violence. We find this word cropping up in journalistic phrases ("street crime" and "street thug"), movie titles (*Mean Streets*), and anti-gang campaigns ("Take back our streets"). Dan's use of the word "street" cites each of these sources from the larger discourse on youths and violence. "Get the gun. Boom!" functions similarly. According to the popular discourse, which sees children as impulsive characters lacking common sense, no sooner would a gun be present among children then it would be fired indiscriminately ("Shoot your friend!").

It's Only a Movie

A response given twice—"It's only a movie" and "it's just a movie"—cites the position of progressive media theorists such as Hodge, Tripp, and Buckingham, who argue that even young children can tell the difference between actual violence and media representations of violence, and that we therefore have little reason to worry that they will imitate the "low-modality" (unrealistic) violence they see in cartoons and action films. The words "just" and "only," which are used by Dan and Jordan to modify "movie," are the key to the meaning here, as they underscore the distinction between movie violence and violence in real life.

The phrase "it's just a movie" also cites a discourse that is much older and more widely known than the modality argument of media researchers. "It's only a movie" was used originally, I believe, to publicize 1950s horror films. Posters and film trailers of this period argued, in effect, "You will see things so real and terrifying in this film that for your own protection, while watching, we recommend you keep saying to yourself, 'It's only a movie. It's only a movie.'" How is it possible for these 11- and 12-year-old children, who have not read Hodge and Tripp's *Children and Television* or Buckingham's *Moving Images* and who are much too young to have seen a trailer for *It Came from Outer Space,* to cite this phrase? Because they are members of a larger discursive community in which phrases such as "it's only a movie" circulate widely, popping up in everyday conversations, sitcom dialogue, talk shows, and various print media. Parents sometimes use the phrase to quell their children's (and their own) fears of disturbing moments in a movie. Indeed, given what must be the millions of phrases children have encountered by age 11, it would be more surprising if they had never heard (and therefore could not strategically deploy) the phrase "It's only a movie."

I Didn't Know It Was Loaded

"Shoot your friend" cites not just our society's belief in the impulsivity of youth but, more specifically, television news reports of children shot and killed by a friend while playing with a gun found in a cabinet or drawer. "Shoot your friend" carries with it intertextual associations to better-known phrases from the coverage of these tragedies, phrases such as "He was too young to know the difference between a real gun and a toy," "We were just playing, and then suddenly it went off" and, of course, "I didn't know it was loaded."

Karate Fighting

"Karate movie" is a reference to the form of violence in the media that is most often singled out these days by educators, parents, and media watchdogs. Just by mentioning "a karate movie," Beau is able to put into play a chain of association of concerns about imitative violence: the effects of *The Mighty Morphin Power Rangers* on preschool-aged children, of martial-arts-inspired Nintendo games ("Street Fighter" and "Ninja Assassin") on elementary school children, and of Bruce Lee, Jean-Claude Van Damme, and Steven Seagal movies on older children and adolescents. Why, of all the forms of violence represented in movies and television, karate (which is very rarely used in actual incidents of violent crime) is the subject of the greatest concern is a question worthy of further investigation. In my experience, boys do a lot of mock karate fighting in school, but when a real fight breaks out, young children rarely use karate moves they have seen on television or in movies. Instead, they punch, grab, twist, scratch, poke, push, or kick in a style one never sees used by a Power Ranger, ninja assassin, or action hero.

Monkey See, Monkey Do

"We just get the soccer ball, throw it at each other" seems to be an exception to the rule that all the answers given to my questions in this segment must be in the form of a formulaic statement about children and imitative violence. But I am inclined to think that this response conforms to the rules of this game. It is an appropriate answer to my question, "When you go to recess, are you going to throw rocks?" In retrospect, I can see that this was a rude question, typical of the way in which teachers and other adults insult and manipulate children by making them reply to questions for which there is only one correct answer. The question invites the singsong, choral response children give when asked if they plan to misbehave: "No, Teacher." For obvious reasons, the children are unlikely to reply, "Yes, we will go out and throw rocks." Here Dan, instead of giving me the predictable, normative reply, "No, we won't throw rocks," cleverly comes up with a way to cite the prevailing discourse about children's suggestibility while not directly implicating himself or his classmates in antisocial behavior. "No. We don't have rocks out there" suggests that the students won't do anything so dangerous as throwing rocks, but only because there aren't any available to throw. In giving this response, Dan thus simultaneously performs and satirizes the notion of the "monkey see, monkey do" child of the media-effects discourse. Beau's follow-up response about throwing soccer balls repeats Dan's suggestion that the students are susceptible to imitative violence. Throwing baseballs wouldn't work here, as baseballs are meant to be thrown. But the soccer ball, which is meant (primarily) to be kicked, becomes a weapon (albeit a not very dangerous one) when thrown. Beau's comment leads us to ask ourselves, "Why would children throw soccer balls during recess unless they had been exposed to some denaturalizing pressure, such as a violent movie?" I find this single statement of Beau's the most convincing remark I got from this group about how watching violent scenes in movies affects their behavior: they do imitate the violence, but in stylized ways that have little chance of causing injury.

Hyped Up, Psyched Up

Beau's sports-and-violence link is picked up again in Dan's phrase, "Like . . . before a game you see a movie or you listen to a kind of song, and it gets you all hyped up." This comment seems to refer to a football custom in which a coach will "psych up" his team by showing them a movie the night before a big game. This is a modern, high-tech version of the old-fashioned inspirational talks a coach delivers before games and at halftime to get his team "psyched." The most famous of these speeches is delivered in a movie— Knute Rockne's locker room speech where he pleads with his Notre Dame team to "Win one for the Gipper" (played by Ronald Reagan, who in turn used this phrase to rally his supporters before a crucial election battle). The use of movies to produce the desired level of pregame psych is described in a *Sports Illustrated* article on a Chicago Bears linebacker:

> [Brian] Cox worships violence. In the basement of his house, he has built a shrine to it—a home theater with a 100-inch screen and two smaller TVs on each side of it—where the day before a game he will watch the goriest movies he can get his Visa on. "To see somebody get stabbed or shot, it kind of gets you excited," Cox once said. If that isn't enough, he puts on the most violent rap music he can find, usually something by Scarface. Soon, Cox is ready to eat bees. ("Losing his head," 1997, p. 55)

An interesting point about the phrase "it gets you all hyped up" is the use of the word "hype." This seems to be a simple mistake—a malapropism, "hyped up" being used incorrectly for the intended, "psyched up"—one contemporary American sports/popular psychology buzz word being confused with another. But "hype" can also be read as an aporia or slip that can give us insight into deeper meaning. "Hype" is an interesting substitution here because it cites a series of media effects issues: the "hype" of the sports entertainment industry, used to get potential viewers to tune in to televised sports (e.g., "Super Bowl hype"); of "hyper" active kids (who supposedly are hyperactive in part because they watch too much TV and play too many violent video games); and of "hypnosis"—which is a very old medium for making people do things they wouldn't do otherwise.

Dan's reference to a pregame film session is a special case of citationality, as he cites two discourses at once (violent sports and movie violence) and, by juxtaposing them, reveals some of their internal contradictions. I asked the group for evidence that watching violent movies can produce violent behavior. Dan cites one of the few examples available in our society of how movies have been used explicitly to stimulate violence: the widespread (and thus presumably effective) practice of showing football players violent films before a game to encourage them to play more violently. This practice is rife with contradictions. Why do we as a society worry that watching stylized representations of violence in movies will make young men violent, but not worry that participating in violent sports will have untoward effects on their behavior off the field? The link between violence in football and violence in real life is supported by the National Football League's practice of hyping its product by stressing the violence of the hits and by the frequent use of martial metaphors by coaches and announcers, who refer to football tactics as "bombs," "blitzes," and "defensive formations" and to players as "troops," "warhorses," and "generals on the field." Given this analogical conflation of sport and war in the larger culture, it is not surprising that many of the children at Koa referred to the Robinson family as "the good team" and the pirates as "the other team" or "the team that was attacking."

WHY THE RELENTLESS CITATIONALITY?

The key question my analysis of this transcript raises is why Stacy, Beau, Dan, and Jordan reply to my questions with a series of citations. One answer would be that this is the nature of communication—everything we say and write cites, copies, mimics, plagiarizes, and/or parodies something someone else has said or written before. This is the position not just of Bakhtin but also of poststructuralist literary theorists, including Jacques Derrida. Extending Saussure's (1959) seminal argument about the nonreferentiality of language, Derrida (1976) argues that words, possessing no inherent meanings, can only be defined with other words. Meaning is thus continually, endlessly deferred. When asked to define what we mean by something we say, all we can do is offer some other words, or cite a dictionary definition, which in turn is circular, as it defines words by giving synonyms. All meaning is thus citational. When asked about imitative violence, the students cite popular arguments from the larger culture. When I ask them to clarify what they mean, they cite other arguments. Such is the nature of language and discourse.

I have attempted to represent the poststructural position here, but I do not fully subscribe to it. Rather than viewing all conversations as nothing but citation and the endless deferral of meaning, I find it more useful to see the relentless citationality of this particular conversation as symptomatic of the particular question I asked here ("Do you think that if you saw a movie like this it might make you more violent?") and the particular context in which the students answered (a media education researcher pulling a group of students out of class to poke his nose into their viewing pleasures). The distinctive feature of the conversational game played by Stacy, Jordan, Beau, and Dan is that every line in this transcript is in the form of a citation, not just to a previously uttered phrase but to phrases that all come from one discourse— the public debate on imitative violence.

The relentless citationality of the students' responses functions to give a sense of circularity and thus of absurdity to the discussion. This circularity and absurdity in turn work to expose the bankrupt nature of the imitative violence debate and also the unseemliness of adults (like me) being so fascinated with the idea that children may be highly susceptible to media violence. I read the relentless citationality here in part as resistance, as a way for these 11- and 12-year-old children to answer my questions without being self-revelatory or self-incriminating. It is a way of simultaneously answering and pleading the Fifth, of rendering themselves opaque by displaying thoughts and concerns that never go beneath the surface.

The citationality here, beyond being a mode of resistance to me, is more importantly a comment on the vacuity of the continuing public and scholarly obsession with the problem of imitative violence. By accurately citing the banalities and clichés of this discourse, Beau, Jordan, Stacy, and Dan's comments, taken collectively, function effectively as critique and parody, echoing and supporting Buckingham's (1996) overview of media effects research: "The major limitation of this enormous body of research—and of the public debates that have largely informed it—has been its almost exclusive preoccupation with the question of imitative violence" (p. 5).

CHILDREN AS BRICOLEURS

My citational analysis of the transcript has demonstrated that children of this age can be quite adept at what French anthropologists (Lévi-Strauss, 1969) and literary theorists call *bricolage,* which they define as a cobbling together of an argument from bits and pieces of discourse circulating in the larger society. As Derrida (1992) writes in his discussion of Claude Lévi-Strauss,

> The bricoleur . . . is someone who uses "the means at hand" which are already there, which had not been especially conceived with an eye to the operation for which they are to be used and to which one tries by trial and error to adapt them, not hesitating to change them whenever it appears necessary, or to try several of them at once, even if their form and their origin are heterogeneous. (p. 157)

The conversation I've analyzed here turns out to be such a work of brico-lage—a pastiche pieced together using a line from a B-movie trailer, a Ronald Reagan campaign slogan, a concept from a scholarly report on media effects on children, a magazine story on how a football player prepares for a game, the voices of morally panicked parents and teachers who fear that children will mindlessly mimic the violence they see in movies, and the socially ex-pected replies of good children reassuring their parents and teachers that they know the difference between right and wrong and between fantasy and reality. The children in this interview are straight-faced as they cite these varied and contradictory statements on imitative violence, thereby making it difficult to read whether they are endorsing or parodying the arguments they re-present. Derrida suggests that when we find a superfluence of signs and citations, as is typical of the work of bricoleurs (including the children whose comments I've analyzed in this chapter), this reflects an absence of underlying meaning. Beau, Stacy, Dan, and Jordan respond to my questions about imitative vio-lence with a plethora of citations not because there is so much they have to share on this topic, but because there is so little. The repetition in their re-sponses reflects the absence of meaning that lies at the core of the concept of imitative violence.

THE EMPTINESS OF THE CONCEPT OF IMITATIVE VIOLENCE

I opened this chapter with a discussion of the methodological difficulties of demonstrating that watching media violence makes children violent. But more basic than this methodological problem is a conceptual problem: the concept of imitative violence just doesn't make much sense. (For a scathing critique of the concept, see Martin Barker's *Ill Effects,* 1997). The discourse of imitative violence is full of sloppy reasoning and half-baked formulations. For example, most discussions of the effects of television on children fail to distinguish between children witnessing actual violence versus watching media representations. This conceptual confusion is captured most clearly in the favorite line of morally panicked media critics, educators, and psychologists who warn parents, "By the time your child is sixteen years old, he will have witnessed twelve thousand killings." Of course, these experts don't really mean killings, they mean representations, many of them highly stylized, as in cartoons and science fiction. And why do we worry so much about the effects on children of watching violent scenes in action movies and cartoons, but so little about their watching violence presented on the television news? Why don't people who are concerned with imitative violence worry more about young children watching "reality television shows"? I am thinking here not only about true crime shows such as *Cops,* but also about the most realistic genre of programs on television: cooking shows where the host, looking right into the camera, says things like, "Take your sharpest knife—make sure it is good and sharp—and then, just like I'm doing, come down hard with a chopping motion." If I subscribed to the concept of imitative violence, I would be more concerned that my young children would run into the kitchen and try cutting something with a sharp knife than that they would shoot someone or throw a coconut bomb.

The imitation in imitative violence is problematic in its own right. There are many ways to imitate violence, and most of them are not dangerous. Children who stage mock karate fights in their living room after watching an episode of *Mighty Morphin Power Rangers* are imitating not just the characters from the show but also the actors, who perform a highly stylized, dance-like imitation of a real fight. To imitate doesn't mean to repeat. Imitation (or, more technically speaking, mimesis) is actually a continuum of practices ranging from impersonation to mimicry, aping, masquerade, caricature, parody, repetition, identification, internalization, and idealization. We need to do more careful studies of how children employ these various forms of mimesis. Yes, children imitate some of the representations of violence they see on TV. But this imitation rarely takes the form of perpetrating actual acts of violence.

One last problem with the concept of imitative violence is that it is characterized by a projection of vulnerability onto others. As Buckingham (1996) writes,

> Effects, it would appear, are things from which other people suffer. We ourselves . . . are somehow immune. . . . These other people are seen as being unable to distinguish between fiction and reality. They are somehow too immature or mentally inadequate to know any better. (p. 65)

Adults thus believe that they are generally immune from imitative violence, but children are susceptible. My interviews confirm Buckingham's findings:

When you ask children about imitative violence, they often tell you that they are immune, but that other, generally younger children are vulnerable. When I asked a group of 9 year-olds at Koa if they were likely to go out on the playground and throw imitation coconut bombs, they told me, "We won't, but the kindergartners might." When I put this question to a group of 10-year-old girls, their response was, "We won't, but the boys will." Thus imitative violence is one of the rarest of diseases: It's a condition that only other people get.

DISTURBING IMAGES

In closing, I should point out that my dismissal of the concept of imitative violence does not mean that I believe that the content of movies is never disturbing to children. Rather, I believe that media researchers' and educators' preoccupation with the problem of imitative violence distracts us from developing more nuanced understandings of the ways in which media content (including, but not limited to, violence) disturbs, confuses, and even traumatizes viewers, young and old. When my children were young, I never saw them imitate the violence of their favorite cartoons or action films in ways that would harm others. But they often were upset by things they watched on television or at the movies, sometimes so much so that they had trouble sleeping at night. The life-threatening perils the family faced in *Swiss Family Robinson* didn't faze my boys, but the death of Bambi's mother and the imprisonment of Dumbo's shook them deeply, as did Pinnochio and his naughty cohorts turning into donkeys. The villains in *G.I. Joe* and *Thundar, the Barbarian* didn't scare my boys in the least, but Sam, my older son, had nightmares for weeks after seeing the trailer for the original *Ghostbusters* when he was 7, and Isaac at 3 was terrified by a PBS documentary on ancient Egypt that featured mummies. If we are to understand the mechanisms by which children come to be disturbed, confused, and misled by media images, we need to move beyond the oversimplification and hyperbole of the concept of imitative violence and attend to the more subtle and varied ways in which individual children interact with specific media texts. Children are affected by media primarily not via imitation, but instead, as we will see in the chapters that follow, through the complex interplay of media content with children's preexisting knowledge, concerns, and anxieties as mediated by their social interactions in specific local communities.

CHAPTER 3

Performing Gender

A group of 11- and 12-year-old girls discussing *Swiss Family Robinson:*

INTERVIEWER: What did you think of that movie?
SANNON: It was junk.
CHERYL: It was a stupid boys' movie.
ANTIONETTE: Why do we have to keep watching boy things?
ALINA: When do we get to watch a girl kind of movie?

Intending to give equal attention to girls' and boys' media issues, I chose movie segments that I thought were balanced in girl and boy themes. But as the girls quoted above point out, I slipped up. In addition to *Swiss Family Robinson*, I showed the children a clip from *The Black Stallion*. Although the protagonists in this film are male (a boy and a stallion), I considered *The Black Stallion* to be more of a girls' than a boys' movie because of girls' love of horses. The focus group discussions confirmed that the film was considerably more popular with girls than with boys, who complained that they shouldn't be made to watch "a junky girls' movie with horses in it." But what I didn't anticipate was that the focus group discussions of *The Black Stallion* would not be as rich or as long as the discussions of *Swiss Family Robinson*. In the transcripts from the 32 focus groups, there were far more comments made about *Swiss Family Robinson* than about *The Black Stallion*.

Why is this the case? One important factor was the ordering of the clips—in each group, we discussed *Swiss Family Robinson* before *The Black Stallion*. By the time we got to *The Black Stallion*, the energy levels of the children and the interviewers tended to flag. In groups where the discussions of *Swiss Family Robinson* were particularly lively or long-winded, we had to foreshorten the discussions of *The Black Stallion* by asking a rapid sequence of questions at the end and rushing the children's replies. Another factor in the skewing of the discussion of the two movies is that the majority of the children, girls as well as boys, didn't like *The Black Stallion* as much as *Swiss Family Robinson*. To be clear: girls liked *The Black Stallion* much more than

31

boys did, but even the girls liked *Swiss Family Robinson* more. I was surprised and a bit distressed by how much the children at Koa enjoyed watching and talking about *Swiss Family Robinson* and how little appreciation they expressed for *The Black Stallion*. I chose *The Black Stallion* not just because I considered it more of a girls' film but because I think it is an excellent movie, lovingly crafted by an outstanding director (Carroll Ballard). *The Black Stallion*, a story of a boy and a horse marooned on a tropical island, is like *Swiss Family Robinson*'s good twin—it is another version of Robinson Crusoe, but with believable characters, compelling problems, laudatory values (except for some unfortunate stereotyping of Arabs, who are the villains in the film), and breathtaking cinematography. And yet the children at Koa (with the notable exception of Shirley, whom you'll meet in this chapter) overwhelmingly preferred *Swiss Family Robinson*. This is a familiar dilemma of teaching and parenting: children often, even usually, prefer movies and television shows we well-meaning adults consider to be inferior or even objectionable to the high-quality programs we would choose for them if they would let us.

GIRLS WITH EACH OTHER AND WITH BOYS

Despite the gender bias that crept into my choice and ordering of movie clips, girls' voices were not silenced in this study. In fact, approximately two-thirds of the responses I quote in this book come from girls. Significantly, the great majority of these comments were made by girls in all-girl focus groups. (Of the 32 focus groups in this study, 8 were all girls, 8 were all boys, and 16 were mixed.) The richest conversations, with the liveliest interchanges among group members, the most spontaneity, and the most open reflection, occurred in the all-girl groups. One implication of this observation would be to take it as an endorsement for all-girl schools, whose proponents argue that such schools give girls a greater opportunity to be themselves, to take intellectual chances, and to play diverse roles. My experience interviewing children at Koa is consistent with the findings of such studies as Myra and David Sadker's (1995) of how girls fare in sex-segregated versus coeducational classrooms. In the Sadkers' research, as in mine, girls in all-girl contexts talk more, follow up more on their intuitions, and are more collaborative than they are when they are with boys.

My impression of the boys, in contrast, is that they acted more or less the same in the all-boy and the mixed-sex groups. Why would girls change the way they present themselves when they are placed in mixed-sex groups while boys stay the same? One explanation would be the power boys enjoy under patriarchy. It is people who are relatively powerless who have to codeswitch and mask their thoughts and feelings when they are in the presence of more powerful people. Girls change the way they speak and act in mixed-sex groups because they must; boys don't change their self-presentation when they move back and forth between all-male and mixed-sex contexts because they don't have to.

But there is an alternative possibility—namely, that the boys are more or less the same in mixed-sex and all-boy groups because they know no other way to be. Like the man who wears the same clothes every day because they are the only clothes he owns, the boys are more or less the same regardless of the composition of the group because this is the only way they know to perform masculinity. Or perhaps they know some other ways, but dare not show them in front of their peers. I have the sense that when talking about popular culture, the boys at Koa, whether they are in the presence of girls or only of their same-sex peers, are under more pressure than the girls to present a narrow range of thoughts and feelings. My thesis in this chapter is that talking about movies and television is a key site for the children at Koa to rehearse and perform gender and that the scripts available for these performances are constraining for girls and even more so for boys.

As Barrie Thorne (1993) and Gail Boldt (1997) point out, when we attend to gender issues we must be alert to the tendency to exaggerate differences between boys and girls. By focusing on hypermasculine boys and hyperfeminine girls, for example, we may fail to notice what is in fact a continuum of gender identities and performances. Thorne cautions against overattending to the "big men" and "big women" of classroom cultures. These are the most charismatic kids of each gender, those who tend to monopolize much of the attention, not only of their peers, but also of teachers and researchers. A misleading circularity can creep into our arguments. We pay inordinate attention to the most highly gendered children and then cite them as evidence for how boys and girls typically behave in school. Boldt's work reminds us that despite the pressure to conform to gender norms, schools are home to gender-bending boys and girls who cannot or will not observe the rules.

In the discussions, several children tended to dominate and several to say very little. In focus group research we inevitably learn more about the thoughts of talkative participants than reserved ones. In the all-girl groups, one or two girls often took control of the conversation. In both coed and all-boy groups, a few boys and their interests and preoccupations tended to dominate. This was especially true in the focus group discussions of the eight-year-olds and up, for whom gender battles were a prevailing theme. With the 5-, 6-, and 7-year-olds, although talk about the different interests of boys and girls was common, arguing and teasing along gender lines were rare. In the discussions among the older children, in contrast, one or two loud, aggressive boys often turned the conversation into an occasion to attack girls' interests and display their own hypermasculine tastes and demeanor.

When I suggest that a few aggressive boys talked the most and set the agenda, I don't mean to imply that the other children in these groups were silenced. Boys with less stereotypically masculine tastes and interests contributed to the discussions, sometimes unobtrusively, by offering insightful comments in quiet voices, sometimes clumsily, in ways that subjected them to scorn and teasing (as, for instance, the 6-year-old boy who volunteered that he sometimes plays with Barbie dolls); and sometimes artfully and bravely, in ways that undercut the dominant boys' displays of machismo (as, for instance, the popular 11-year-old boy who sided with the girls in his group in preferring dramas and sitcoms to action films). And girls in mixed-sex focus groups often held their own. In these groups, although girls generally were unable to control the terms of the debate, they were able to marshal arguments in defense of their interests and positions. The gender battles appeared to exact a toll on the girls. In the combative mixed-sex discussions, girls didn't enjoy the freedom and range they had in all-girl groups to play various roles, to be playful, silly, reflective, and self-revelatory. Instead, they were often forced to defend their interests and tastes against the boys' attacks. In these groups the girls tended to laugh and joke less, and their posture and demeanor were defensive, their bodies much more guarded than in the all-girl groups, where they frequently playfully teased each other, threw their heads back in laughter, and even got up out of their chairs to dance. Children live in two worlds at school—one that is sex-segregated, the other coeducational. As Thorne describes, on the playground, at lunch, and when teachers let them form their own groups, elementary school children gravitate toward same-sex peers. At other times in the school day, boys and girls are compelled to interact.

GENDER PLAY

To highlight the issue of gender performance, I focus in this chapter on one extended conversation from a mixed group of boys and girls aged eight and nine. In this conversation, the war between the sexes was especially heated. Yet the tensions that arose in this group were typical of the gender teasing and positioning that went on in nearly all of the mixed-sex focus groups of kids 8 years old and up. The transcript I analyze in this chapter works as a sustained piece of drama: there are strong characters, primal conflicts, plot twists, foreshadowing, and reiteration of key themes. As in many of Shakespeare's plays, there is even an effective mirroring of the protagonists' positions in the supporting characters. My analysis draws on the concept of performance in both common senses of the term: The children's comments can be read more usefully as attempts to perform gender than as markers of preexisting, stable gender identities they bring to the conversation, and the transcript becomes more meaningful when we approach it as a sustained piece of drama rather than as a collection of discrete statements.

The participants in this discussion are three girls (Jewel, Harlynn, and Shirley) and three boys (Frank, Branson, and Clem) from a combined third- and fourth-grade classroom.

INTERVIEWER: What's your favorite movie or television show?
JEWEL: *Full House.*
HARLYNN: Um, I like, ah, ah . . .
INTERVIEWER: You can't decide? That's okay. How about, if you think of one, I'll come back to you later?
SHIRLEY: My favorite is *Black Stallion.*
FRANK: *Predator.*
BRANSON: Bart Simpson.
CLEM: Mine's *Terminator II.*

These opening comments introduce a theme of gender difference in tastes and sensibilities that will be maintained throughout the discussion. Jewel's choice is a television sitcom about a family, featuring a cute little girl. Shirley, not knowing that we are about to show her a clip from *The Black Stallion*, coincidentally nominates it as her favorite. Frank and Clem choose violent thrillers starring Arnold Schwarzenegger. Branson comes up with "Bart Simpson." By responding with the name of a character from *The Simpsons* rather than with the show's title, Branson seems to suggests that he identifies with Bart Simpson, who is known for his naughty wit, his fights with his brainy sister, and his interest in popular culture. At any rate, throughout this interview Branson will play the Bart Simpson role—funny, sarcastic, provocative, but fundamentally decent and capable of empathy (even toward a girl).

Following a brief discussion of the *Teenage Mutant Ninja Turtles* and Cheerios commercials, we asked them to list the commercials they liked best:

SHIRLEY: Barbie.
BRANSON and *CLEM* [making faces]: Ew.
FRANK: *T2.*
CLEM: Ones with violence.
INTERVIEWER: Do you want what you see on commercials?
BRANSON: Most of the time. Unless it's something for girls.
INTERVIEWER: What kind of commercial interests you?
SHIRLEY: Livestock.
BRANSON: She likes Barbie horses.

SHIRLEY: No, livestock. Real horse commercials.
FRANK: She loves horses.
BRANSON: She loves real horse commercials.
CLEM: She said she'd kiss a horse's butt when I teased her. I said "Go kiss
    a cat." She goes, "I'd rather kiss a horse's butt."
SHIRLEY: I never said—
BRANSON: —She said she'd rather, she didn't say she would.

In this early stage of the conversation, gender lines are drawn. Branson
and Clem begin teasing Shirley in a manner that will continue throughout
the interview. The boys first express their disgust for Barbie, which Shirley
nominates as her favorite commercial, and then make fun of Shirley's interest
in horses. In their discussion of kissing a horse's butt, the children cite an
earlier conversation, which I imagine went something like this:

SHIRLEY: I love animals.
CLEM: Then go kiss a cat.
SHIRLEY: I'd rather kiss a horse's butt than kiss a cat.

By referring to an earlier incident, Shirley and Clem let us know that they
have a teasing relationship that exists outside the context of the focus group
interview. In my experience, this sort of teasing about love and kissing is
characteristic of the way American boys and girls banter at this age. On *Pee-
Wee's Playhouse,* Pee Wee Herman captured the spirit of this talk with his
joke, "If you love peanut butter so much, why don't you marry it?" These
conversations about love and kissing are clearly silly and thus a relatively
safe way for children to begin to talk about desire, sexuality, and gender
difference.

Rhetorical sparring and legalistic wrangling also are typical of talk at
this age. Clem boasts of having caught Shirley in a verbal trap by challenging
her to kiss a cat. Branson, in this instance, breaks gender ranks and takes on
the role of Shirley's defense attorney. I understand him to be saying, "She
didn't say she would kiss a horse's butt. She said, given the choice between
kissing a cat on the lips or a horse's butt, she would choose the horse's butt."
The distinction Branson makes here may seem like hairsplitting, but it is a
kind of argumentation that children relish at this age.

GENDERED REACTIONS TO VIOLENCE AND SPECIAL EFFECTS

The children next were shown the clip from *Swiss Family Robinson*:

BRANSON: Yeah, I saw this one.
FRANK: Too bad you don't have *Predator I.*

CLEM: There's a little kid.

BRANSON: I remember that. Boom!

FRANK: He's the king.

JEWEL: Uh-oh.

[Branson and Frank mime bomb-throwing techniques.]

CLEM [as the pile of logs is released]: Oh, chopsticks!

HARLYNN: Oh, he's getting runned over!

BRANSON: Yeah, I saw this one.

CLEM: That guy looks like in *Street Fighter*.

FRANK: Yeah, *Street Fighter* rules. I'm gonna get Super NES. I already got Gameboy, Nintendo, and Sega, all I need is Super NES.

BRANSON: Oh, I have two Gameboys, Nintendo, Super NES, so all I need is Turbical Graphics and Sega Genesis.

CLEM: Oh, yeah. That's all I need, too.

INTERVIEWER: We're not here to talk about video games. I want to hear what you think about the movie.

FRANK: It was good. They had so much traps.

BRANSON: It was funny.

CLEM: Tiger, tiger.

BRANSON: I liked the part with the bombs. KABOOM!

FRANK: If you had kept it running . . . I liked it when the tiger ate the guy.

INTERVIEWER: Do you think it was real or made up?

SHIRLEY: Made up.

INTERVIEWER: Why?

BRANSON: 'Cause I don't think there is something such as cherry bombs or coconut bombs.

SHIRLEY: There is, you just fill 'em up with gunpowder.

CLEM: Yeah, you just put in gunpowder.

INTERVIEWER: Do you think that could really happen?

FRANK: Yeah.

CLEM: They couldn't do that. Especially the chopsticks. They had to be foam.

BRANSON: Yeah. They bounced back up. They were still alive when they did that.

SHIRLEY: Yeah. They fell and bounced.

BRANSON: And the rocks. They just fell on them but they didn't care, they just kept walking.

JEWEL: Some people looked like they were bleeding.

CLEM: Some, it looked like when a person threw a cherry bomb, instead of him flying up with the cherry bomb it was like he was jumping.

BRANSON: Yeah, because before the cherry bomb even hit the ground he jumped.

FRANK: It's not a cherry bomb; it's a coconut bomb.

In this segment of the discussion, the boys dominated the conversation with their excited talk about the violence in the scene, their knowledge of special effects, and their bragging about the toys they have or soon hope to get. The great interest Clem, Frank, and Branson take in the bombs and logs ("chopsticks") is typical of the way boys talked about movies across the groups. The boys clearly are excited by and interested in the violence in movies. When we examine their statements, we see that the core of their interest isn't in real violence but in how movies and other media represent violence using various special effects. For instance, Branson and Clem make insightful connections between how modality and character issues are handled in Disney's *Swiss Family Robinson* and Nintendo's *Street Fighter*. Clem observes that a character in the movie (he seems to be referring to either the pirate king or the bald pirate) reminds him of a character from *Street Fighter* (probably the sumo wrestler E-Honda, who is shirtless and big like the bald pirate and has Kabuki-style eye makeup like the pirate leader). This is an interesting intertextual association, as it points out that both *Swiss Family Robinson* and violent video games have violent Asian characters. But there is also an important difference. The Asian characters in *Swiss Family Robinson* are buffoonish oafs taken from Hollywood's stable of interchangeable villains. In contrast, differentiated Asian characters are prominent in video games such as *Street Fighter* because these games were originally developed in Japan for a Japanese audience, and because the best-known martial arts were invented in Asia.

In contrast to *Swiss Family Robinson*, in *Street Fighter* and *Mortal Kombat,* most of the Asian characters are attractive. While we might find the violence of video games disturbing, these globally circulating games give local children in places like Koa the opportunity to identify with characters across racial and gender lines—a positive feature of video game playing that merits more study. We need studies, for example, that would help us understand the significance of boys playing video games in which the character they choose to play (or, as they put it, to "be") is a Chinese female. As we learn later in the discussion, the *Street Fighter* character most admired by Clem, Branson, and Frank is Chun-Li, the female martial arts expert. I suspect that many boys and girls choose to play/be Chun-Li not only because of her prowess (her "special moves"), but also because they identify with her smallness and litheness, compared to her much larger, more muscular opponents.

The connection Clem makes between violent video games and *Swiss Family Robinson* reflects not only a similarity in the characters in these two genres but also the similar questions action movies and video games raise about modality and effects. Much of the marketing of video games and game platforms centers on their claims to realism. The games make rapid and continuous progress in rendering the human form and acts of violence in ways that are perceived to be increasingly believable, which means, ironically, not lifelike so much as movie-like. Action movies, in turn, often attempt to present fight scenes that have the look and feel of video games. *Street Fighter* and *Mortal Kombat* are video games that have been turned into movies. Branson's and Clem's comments about Nintendo machines and *Street Fighter* thus can be read in two ways: on one hand, as a familiar example of the way boys interrupt the flow of discussions to talk about their toys; on the other hand, as insightful observations on how video games and movies use special effects to represent violence in stylized but realistic ways.

In this discussion, except for Shirley's comment about how one could make a coconut bomb out of gunpowder, the conversation about special effects was dominated by the boys. In most of the focus group discussions of *Swiss Family Robinson*, boys had much more to say than girls about the realism of the film's violence. This gender difference can be interpreted in several ways. One possibility is that the boys at Koa, compared to the girls, have a greater interest in and knowledge of the physical and mechanical world. Educators concerned with the underrepresentation of girls in higher-level mathematics and science classes have speculated that the greater access to the world of machines and projectiles (skateboards, cars, balls, and bullets) enjoyed by boys in our society may be a key contributing factor (Tobias, 1990). Many of the boys' comments on *Swiss Family Robinson* have to do with physics, specifically with the question of how various kinds of objects, with various masses, shapes, and densities, fly, bounce, and impact the things (or people) they hit: "They had to be foam." "They bounced back up." "They fell and bounced." "The rocks bounced, too." Across the groups, "plastic" (and other synthetic polymers) came up again and again in the discussions: "Those rocks was probably plastic." "Those weren't real logs—I bet they were plastic." "Those logs didn't look heavy—the way they was bouncing, you could tell they were styrofoam." *Plastic* is a word with many meanings, including "malleable," "synthetic," and "insincere." In the discussions at Koa, it was most often used as a synonym for "fake" or "unrealistic." Thus, when boys in several of the groups commented that the rocks and logs were plastic, I think they were suggesting not only that these objects behaved more like lightweight polymers than like rock or wood, but also that they found the film to be unrealistic. I read Clem's description of the logs as "chopsticks" as referring obliquely to the Asianness of the pirates but more directly to the fact that the logs in the scene are like disposable chopsticks in being made of a kind of wood so light that it doesn't feel or behave like real wood.

For the older boys at Koa, movies with fantastic science fiction plots but high-quality special effects (such as *Terminator II*) are judged to be more real and compelling than movies with more plausible plots but "junky" special effects (such as *Swiss Family Robinson*). As a fifth-grade boy admonished us,

"You should have showed us something good, like *T2* or *Die Hard*, instead of these junk movies that are so fake." The older boys at Koa critiqued the lack of realism of *Swiss Family Robinson* by pointing to the cheapness of the special effects, the awkwardness of the stunt work, and the physical implausibility of the action: "Instead of him flying up with the cherry bomb, it was like he was jumping." "Yeah, because before the bomb even hit the ground, he jumped." "They just fell on them, but they didn't care; they just kept walking." Girls, in contrast, tended to evaluate the realism of the film by attending to the implausibility of the plot, the lack of character development, and genre considerations, as we can see in the comments of a group of 10- and 11-year-old girls:

INTERVIEWER: What did you think about it?

ANTIONETTE: Exciting.

SANNON: But the thing about it, everything goes right. It's kind of phony.

INTERVIEWER: So would you say this movie is real or made-up?

TINA: If it was real, sometimes it won't work. You have to have a plan, but then if that plan don't work, then you go to Plan B, and if it don't work, well . . . But in this movie everything they planned worked too good the first time.

INTERVIEWER: Who were the good guys?

SEVERAL GIRLS TOGETHER: The Robinsons.

INTERVIEWER: How could you tell?

CHERYL: You could kind of tell by the way they acted. The good guys acted like a family and the bad guys acted like pirates.

ANTIONETTE: Yeah, the bad guys, you could tell by how they were dressed, and what they were doing, and how they were acting.

SANNON: In this kind of movie it's easy to tell, but in mysteries sometimes you can't tell. If this was a mystery, the bad guy could even be the dad.

ALINA: I think the movie's kind of fake, because the good guys in real life wouldn't be fighting. They would run away if it was real.

The girls attribute the film's lack of realism less to its lame special effects than to its implausible plot—all of the Robinsons' tricks work too perfectly—and to the lack of character complexity—goodness and badness in the film can be read too easily, unlike in a mystery, where, as in real life, people's underlying character is harder to read in their dress or visible behavior.

The older girls at Koa tended to respond to the violence in *Swiss Family Robinson* not as their male peers did, with critiques of the stunts and special effects, but with expressions of horror and sympathy. The opportunity to react publicly to movie violence provided the boys and girls at Koa with a stage on which to perform gender. When asked about their reactions to the representations of violence in *Swiss Family Robinson*, the older boys claimed that they were neither scared nor concerned. Boys performed masculinity by demonstrating their knowledge of the physical world ("rocks don't bounce like that") and of movie-making ("they use, like, trampoline things to make the bodies fly around like that") and by claiming that it takes something much more gruesome and realistic than *Swiss Family Robinson* to excite or faze them ("I've seen lots of much more violent movies like *Aliens* and *Terminator* and *Friday the 13th*"). In contrast, the girls tended to perform femininity with statements of empathy for the victims of film violence and demonstrations that they are easily and strongly affected by representations of violence and gore, as we can see in the comments of a group of 10- and 11-year-old girls:

INTERVIEWER: What do you think about it?

LIA: It's very, very, very scary. And funny. And interesting.

INTERVIEWER: What part was the scary part?

LIA: When they fell down into the tiger.

INTERVIEWER: How did it make you feel?

LIA [shivering]: Gives you the chills.

TASHA: The scary part for me was when the logs came down and went on top of them, and they were all dead. [Shaking and hugging herself] Ew.

INTERVIEWER: Is this a real story or a made-up one?

SHAUNA: Make-believe!

INTERVIEWER: How do you know it was make-believe?

SHAUNA: Because in real life the logs would have killed them.

TASHA: I don't think they would kill people like that.

LIA: Maybe that's just pumped-in air.

INTERVIEWER: How did you feel when the logs came rolling down the hill?

LIA: Oooh, that feels nervous. Ooooh. [Makes shivering motions]

SHAUNA: Like it hurts.

TASHA: Like I wanted to run away.

DANIA: Yeah. I don't want to die.

INTERVIEWER: How did you feel when the coconuts exploded?

DANIA: Eeew!

LIA: Scaaared.

INTERVIEWER: So is that movie really upsetting?

TASHA: Not really.

LIA: No, not really.

Several things are going on here that merit comment. I've argued that girls at Koa generally had less to say than boys about special effects and stunts. And yet the girls in this group demonstrate that they are well aware of the lack of realism of the movie's effects ("In real life the logs would have killed them." "That's just pumped-in air."). Perhaps the girls at Koa are as capable of critically evaluating technical effects in films as the boys are, but don't feel so compelled to show off their mastery of this domain of knowledge. In my experience, females seem to feel less urgency than males do to talk authoritatively about things they understand imperfectly. Another noteworthy feature of this passage is that it is clear that the girls are performing, rather than revealing, a susceptibility to movie violence. These girls are putting on a show of being horrified. Their expressions of horror are highly theatrical, as they mix fake screams, sighs, and moans with references to "the chills" and dramatic recreations of the somatic effects they claim the film had on them (shivering, shaking, clutching themselves). At the end of this passage, they suddenly drop out of character and admit to the interviewer that they weren't actually upset by the movie: "So is that movie really upsetting?" "No, not really."

It is worth noting that these girls performed femininity in the absence of a male audience (the interviewer for this group was a female graduate student). Across the single-sex focus groups, boys consistently performed stereotypical versions of masculinity and girls of femininity, even though no peer of the opposite sex was present. How might we explain this? One explanation for the gender performativity in the single-sex groups would be that girls and boys use same-sex audiences to rehearse performances of gender to be used later to attract the opposite sex. However, there are some problems with this explanation. I have no doubt that children sometimes practice on their friends patterns of gender performance and intimacy that they will use in romantic relationships when they are older. But to read childhood as a rehearsal for adulthood is to fail to appreciate and acknowledge that children's words, actions, and relationships are meaningful and significant in the here and now (Leavitt, 1994). The way the children at Koa talk about and enact gender is not a dress rehearsal—it is the performance, a performance that is as complete and meaningful as any that will follow in adulthood (Boldt, 1997). Reading the same-sex interactions of childhood as a rehearsal for intimacy with someone of the opposite sex in adulthood is also myopically heteronormative—all children don't grow up to be heterosexuals, and same-sex intimacy is not something everyone grows out of when they become adults. A better explanation for the gender performativity in the single-sex discussion groups would be that gender performances are intended at least as much for the same sex as for the opposite sex. Boys know that if they fail to appear rigorously male in their interests and demeanor in front of other males, the repercussions are more severe than if such a failure were to take place in front of girls. As Buckingham (1993) observed of the boys in his study, "There was often a mutual policing going on, in which boys who stepped out of line were reprimanded or humiliated" (p. 268). And many women report that they dress more to impress other women (who are more expert readers of the semiotics of dress) than men (on whom nuances of dress often are wasted).

I suggest that in their discussions of the violence in *Swiss Family Robinson*, the older children are performing not just gender but also sexuality. By appearing to be unfazed by screen violence, the boys demonstrate a version of toughness/hardness that is associated with virility. In our culture, a man's ability to control his feelings of fear and horror functions metonymically as a sign of sexual competence. In popular culture, male icons from James Bond to the Fonz are cool and collected, unfazable and unflappable, whether they are confronted with a threat of violence or the chance to have sex with an attractive woman. Many of the older boys at Koa affected this worldly, detached demeanor in the discussions of *Swiss Family Robinson*. The older girls at Koa, in contrast, by demonstrating in words, expressions, and gestures that they are easily and deeply moved by screen violence, performed a stylized, culturally constructed version of female sexual arousability. In our culture, to be moved readily and visibly by violence and horror (and also by nature and art) is metonymically associated with being a sexually desirable/desiring woman. This is an association that Jane Austen explored (and satirized) in *Sense and Sensibility* through the character of Marianne, who is too easily, but charmingly, moved and excited. It is an association that Freud explored in his studies of his hysterical female patients, whose sexual urges were too readily somatized. The association of being horrified with being sexually excited also contributes, I believe, to the moral panic surrounding screen violence—as a society we're worried not just that boys will be desensitized by watching horror, but also that girls somehow will become overstimulated. This is a dynamic that is well understood by adolescent boys and girls, who know that horror films work well as makeout movies.

I am not suggesting that the girls at Koa who put on a show of squealing and swooning and being scared by the mild violence in *Swiss Family Robinson* were knowingly or intentionally mimicking female sexual arousal. Rather, I am suggesting that watching and talking about movies with a group of peers is a context in which it is inevitable that children will perform versions of masculinity and femininity that circulate in the larger society. Children live their lives amid a swirl of contradictory notions of sex and gender. Out of this confusion, girls and boys cobble together performative identities as females and males. An important aspect of gendered identity is sexuality. Well before puberty, children imitate and perform versions of what it means to be sexually desirable and competent adults. These mimetic performances of sexuality, which I believe are inevitable, become dangerous only when they are forced on children inappropriately by adults (I'm thinking here, for example, of the sexuality of the "Little Miss" beauty pageants, which are orchestrated by and for adults), or when children's playful performances of gender roles are misread as sexual invitation or provocation by adult sexual predators.

Public performances of masculine and feminine film viewing should not be mistaken for what males and females actually think and feel when they watch violent movies. I can videotape children in focus group discussions performing masculinity and femininity, but these videotapes can't tell us what goes on in the hearts and minds of child movie-viewers. As Carol Clover argues in *Men, Women, and Chainsaws* (1992), male and female reactions to cinematic representations of violence are very complex, involving gender performativity, projective identification (which often crosses gender lines), and cycles of emotional buildup and release. Girls at Koa generally acted more disturbed by the violence in *Swiss Family Robinson* than did boys. But I suspect that many of the boys were more bothered by the representations of violence and many of the girls less so than they claimed in the discussions. For example, although the boys announced that they found the special effects in *Swiss Family Robinson* primitive and too babyish for their tastes, the videotape of them watching the action scene from the movie shows them to be enthralled.

GENDER WARS

For many of the older boys, appearing to be normatively gendered involved not just displaying male interests and having a masculine demeanor but also disparaging girls and their interests. Branson, Clem, and Frank began this sort of oppositional defining of masculinity when we asked their group to explain who were the good guys and who were the bad guys:

BRANSON: The bad guys were the pirates and the good guys were up in the cave-rock.
INTERVIEWER: How could you tell the good guys from the bad guys?
CLEM: The good guys were the only family there, and the bad guys had more people.
INTERVIEWER: How do you know they were bad guys?
BRANSON: They were pirates, and I saw that movie before.
INTERVIEWER: Did you see any girl pirates?
FRANK: No.
INTERVIEWER: Why is that?
BRANSON: Because it was a tough job. Like, 'cause, they would die fast.
SHIRLEY: There were too some girls.

CLEM: Not Chun-Li. She wouldn't die. She would get 'em [mimes karate-
fighting].
BRANSON: Yeah, Chun-Li. Give me five, brah! [slaps hands with Clem]

The gender battle is joined with Branson's comment that the girls "would die
fast." Shirley defends her sex by retorting, in the familiar register of children's contrarian argumentation, "There were too some girls." This comment
seems to be a non sequitur. What is in question here is not the presence of
female characters in the movie but the absence of female pirates, or, more
generally, of women who can fight. But I think Shirley is responding not to
the literal meaning of Branson's comment but to the deeper implication that
girls lack agency. When Shirley says, "There were too some girls," I think
she is announcing that "girls, too, have agency" and letting the boys know
that she isn't going to be silent in the face of their misogynistic posturing. In
a departure from the norm of gender solidarity, Clem challenges Branson's
suggestion that girls can't fight by saying, "Not Chun-Li. She wouldn't die.
She would get 'em." Chun-Li, a character from *Street Fighter,* is a female
who can fight. Reestablishing the norm of masculine solidarity, Branson invites Clem to do a high five in a macho tribute (ironically) to their shared
identification with Chun-Li.

Clem's citation of a female action hero effectively diffused the gender
battle that was about to break out between Branson and Shirley. But this
avoidance of hostilities turned out to be fleeting, as we see in the next section
of the transcript, which begins with the comments the children made while
watching the clip from *The Black Stallion*:

CLEM: *Black Stallion*! Shirley's favorite.
[Shirley smiles and nods in acknowledgment]
FRANK: Oh, I seen this.
CLEM: I read about it.
[videotape ends]
INTERVIEWER: What did you think of that one?
FRANK: Junk.
CLEM: Boring.
SHIRLEY: Good!
BRANSON: Only girls like it 'cause mostly girls like horses and animals.
SHIRLEY: What about cowboys?
CLEM: They shoot them and kill them.
SHIRLEY: They don't kill them! They ride them to cut calves.
CLEM: They kill them.

As *The Black Stallion* tape begins to play, Clem points out and Shirley acknowledges that this is her favorite movie. Shirley's love of *The Black Stallion* and more generally of everything to do with horses is so well known in this community that it serves as a ready target for the boys' derision. By refusing to hide or downplay her interests and desires, Shirley makes herself vulnerable to displays of misogynistic male bonding.

Frank and Clem start the trouble by stating that Shirley's favorite movie is "junk" and boring. Branson makes the terms of the argument clear: this is a movie that only girls could like, as it is about animals. Shirley, not about to back down, cleverly counters by introducing the example of cowboys. This statement is an enthymeme, a syllogism whose central assumptions need not be expressed within an interpretive community (Fish, 1982) because they are implied: cowboys are masculine icons, and cowboys are bonded with their horses and care for cattle, so it is patently untrue to suggest that only girls like horses and animals. But Shirley's logic provokes Clem to raise the terms of the attack by replying, "They shoot them and kill them." While I am inclined to agree with Clem that cowboys, compared to little girls, tend to be unsentimental about horses, I find his argument that cowboys shoot and kill animals to be unfair and mean-spirited. As Shirley points out, cowboys don't kill horses, they use them to take care of cattle. Clem knows that Shirley is very much identified with horses, so when he suggests that there are men who kill horses, he alludes to the power males wield over females by the use or threat of use of violence.

While this example may seem extreme, in my experience at Koa and elsewhere, it is one of the typical discourses boys and girls employ to perform gender. Girls perform femininity by expressing both identification with and sympathy toward animals. Boys perform masculinity not only by mocking girls' interest in cute animals but also by joking about and occasionally committing acts of cruelty toward animals. This is one of the unlikable preadolescent male traits satirized on *Beavis and Butt-head*. The association of masculinity with hunting and blood sports and of femininity and childhood with tenderheartedness toward animals is a very old and well-established cultural pattern that children are drawn into as they attempt to establish their gendered identities. Many of the boys at Koa write in their journals about the first time they went pig hunting or deep-sea fishing with their dads or other male relatives. One step in the transition from being a little to a big boy is the switch from a childlike and feminine tenderheartedness toward animals to a more masculine position. This transition is complex because there are several masculine positions for boys to choose from, ranging from being disinterested in animals, to being unsentimental and utilitarian in using and controlling them, to adopting a reverent, respectful attitude toward the animals they hunt and kill, to dominating animals (dogs in particular) through patriarchal power (the firm hand of the benevolent master), to being sadistic toward animals.

The position Clem performs at this point in the discussion is one of provocative meanness, not just toward animals but also toward Shirley. It might seem harsh to suggest that an 8-year-old boy is misogynistic. But, as Valerie Walkerdine argues in "Sex, Power, and Pedagogy" (1990), in certain contexts even very young boys can wield the power of patriarchy over girls and grown women. I would point out, however, that there is an important if subtle difference between being a misogynist and making misogynistic statements in a media discussion with peers. As we've seen throughout this book, children perform various roles and try on various positionalities as they discuss movies. Because it is very difficult from observing their performances to read children's underlying thoughts and feelings, we can't tell from Clem's comment here what he actually thinks and feels about Shirley and other girls. Shirley doesn't appear to be terribly bothered or hurt by Clem's comment, which might suggest that their exchange has an element of playfulness we miss when we use labels such as misogyny. Rather than viewing Clem and Shirley's interaction as an example of male hostility to females, we might instead conceptualize their conversation as being a dyadic gender performance that boys and girls voluntarily play, like chasing games on the playground. As Barrie Thorne (1993) writes of these games and other forms of what she calls "gender-boundary play":

> They are accompanied by stylized forms of action, a sense of performance, mixed and ambiguous meanings (the situations often teeter between play and aggression, and heterosexual meanings lurk within other definitions), and by an array of intense emotions—excitement, playful elation, anger, desire, shame, and fear. (p. 66)

The scripts of these games, if taken out of context, would suggest that boys are the perpetrators and girls their unwilling victims. But such an interpretation misses the excitement and pleasure children of both sexes often experience in these games, and it also robs girls of agency and positions them in the role of helpless victims of patriarchy.

At any rate, as we turn back to the discussion of *The Black Stallion*, we find the gender war heating up, as Frank, Branson, and Clem continue to perform masculinity by putting down feminine interests and claiming to be interested in violence and nudity:

INTERVIEWER: Do you think that was a good movie?
SHIRLEY: Yeah.
FRANK: No.

HARLYNN: Kind of.

BRANSON: Boring.

CLEM: Ba-ba-ba-boring.

JEWEL: If something happened it would be more exciting.

INTERVIEWER: How could you tell from that short part that you didn't like it?

BRANSON: 'Cause I don't like horses.

CLEM: I don't like stallions.

INTERVIEWER: What makes a good movie?

BRANSON: Action, violence.

CLEM: Yeah, violence.

FRANK: Blood.

BRANSON: Bad language. Adult situations. And nudity.

CLEM: Nudity, yeah! [exchanges high fives with Branson]

BRANSON: On pay-per-view I see nudity.

SHIRLEY: Pay-per-view! That has Playboy on it!

CLEM: I like action. I like violence. I like rated-R movies.

FRANK: I seen *Cliffhanger*!

BRANSON: That's what I watch.

SHIRLEY: He watches Playboy movies!

JEWEL: My brother says that on public TV they have naked people and they call it education.

INTERVIEWER: Is that what he says? Hm. What about you girls, what do you think makes a good movie?

HARLYNN: Funny.

JEWEL: Character.

SHIRLEY: Horses.

JEWEL: A happy ending.

FRANK: I like a lot of blood.

CLEM: Yeah! That's the way!

FRANK: Yeah, like in *Predator I*, he shoots these laser beams and they go right through this guy.

BRANSON: I like everything except comedy. I like if the movie is not funny and not a comedy unless it is funny enough or in a violent way.

CLEM: I like *Terminator II*. I like blood. I like violence. I like shooting.

BRANSON: Yeah!

INTERVIEWER: What kind of movie was that?

SHIRLEY: Horse story.

BRANSON: Passion.

CLEM: Which I hate.

I find the performances of masculinity in this section to be highly theatrical and thus not entirely convincing. One clue is the singsong cadence and litany-like phrasing used by Branson when he says "Bad language. Adult situations. And nudity." This is repeated (twice) later in the transcript by Clem when he says, "I like action. I like violence. I like rated-R movies" and "I like *Terminator II*. I like blood. I like violence. I like shooting." These statements are more highly stylized and poetically structured than children's ordinary speech. And by using the non-childlike terms "bad language," "nudity," "passion," "pay-per-view," and "adult situations," Branson lets us know that he is citing/performing an adult social discourse about movies and gender as opposed to speaking earnestly about his own tastes and interests. The boys' playful repetition (almost chanting) of the words "violence" and "blood" throughout the conversation works simultaneously to express and parody the position of the stereotypical male filmgoer. I am suggesting not that the boys don't actually enjoy films such as *Terminator II*, which has lots of fighting and a little blood, but that in addition to genuinely enjoying such films, they are enjoying performing the part of bloodthirsty action-film addicts. To the boys, the flip side of liking blood and violence in movies is scorning passion and romance. But by announcing that they hate passion, instead of communicating mature masculinity the boys come across as, well, little boys, who despite their claim to be interested in nudity and adult situations, find kissing yucky and sexual attraction mystifying.

The girls don't have much to say in this section of the interview. I suspect this is partly because the boys are so intent on dominating the conversation with their shows of masculinity and partly because of the three girls, only Shirley likes *The Black Stallion* enough to be willing to defend it. The comments the girls do make here suggest to me that they, like the boys, are performing more than revealing how they feel about movies. I don't doubt that these girls like movies with well-drawn characters and happy endings. But their language here, like the boys', is unnatural—when the interviewer asks them what they like in a movie, they reply in the style of good girls answering questions in a language arts class ("Character," "A happy ending"). Shirley has been unable to mask her pleasure in horses and horse movies, but Jewel and Harlynn, unwilling to make themselves so vulnerable, use familiar classroom responses to avoid revealing much about their moviegoing pleasures and desires.

The situation grew even more difficult for Shirley in the next section of the discussion, when the interviewer asked some follow-up questions about *The Black Stallion*:

INTERVIEWER: It's kind of hard to judge a movie when you see just a little
  bit, yeah? Have any of you watched the whole thing?
BRANSON: Yeah.
CLEM: Yes, and it was boring.

SHIRLEY: I have *Black Stallion* and *Black Stallion Returns*. *Black Stallion Returns* was better.

CLEM: She loves horses because she rides them.

HARLYNN: Don't make fun of her.

INTERVIEWER: So do the rest of you think this would be a good movie if you watched the whole thing?

FRANK: No.

CLEM: It was boring.

HARLYNN: No.

SHIRLEY: Don't copy them.

JEWEL: Maybe. I never saw it before, so . . .

SHIRLEY: Yes you did, you saw it with me!

JEWEL: No, I didn't.

SHIRLEY [appealing to the interviewer]: She did! She saw it at my party! [turning to Jewel] You saw the whole thing. You went to my party. You were there!

JEWEL: But I didn't watch . . .

SHIRLEY: Yes, you did. Why are you saying you didn't?

Shirley's feeling of being abandoned by her friends and gender-mates is heartbreaking. She pleads with Harlynn and Jewel not to side with the boys' disparagement of *The Black Stallion* and thus, by implication, of girls' interests. But Shirley's interest in horses and love of *The Black Stallion* is beyond the female norm. To side with her in this argument is to put oneself in a position to be teased and mocked. Shirley feels that Harlynn and Jewel have betrayed her (and the girls' team) by feigning disinterest in *The Black Stallion*. But we could also argue that from her friends' perspective, it is Shirley who is letting down the side by being so extreme in her interests and so unstrategic in revealing areas of vulnerability to the enemy.

BOYS' VULNERABILITY

In the last section of this interview the children were asked to discuss what they know about the mechanics of movie-making, in anticipation of the video production curriculum that is about to begin:

INTERVIEWER: If we were to make a movie, what jobs would we need?

JEWEL: Director.

SHIRLEY: If we make *The Black Stallion*, someone's gotta be the horse.

FRANK: I'm not making *Black Stallion*.

BRANSON: *Terminator*!

CLEM: I'm not gonna be no black stallion.
FRANK: Navigator.
JEWEL: Narrator.
BRANSON: Picture person.
FRANK: Sounds.
CLEM: Actors.
JEWEL: Writer.
FRANK: Drawer.
JEWEL: Illustrator.
BRANSON: Creator.
CLEM: Cameraman.

Here, at the end of the interview, when the conversation shifts from the consumption to the production of movies, the power balance of the gender war suddenly shifts. Jewel, who will prove to be one of the more talented children at Koa in video production, takes the lead in this conversation by listing "director" as the most important job in movie-making and by correcting Clem's suggestion of "navigator" and Frank's of "drawer," supplying the correct technical terms "narrator" and "illustrator." Shirley, beaten but unbowed, suggests that they should begin thinking about making a version of *The Black Stallion*. Perhaps it is the bossy register Shirley adopts and particularly her use of the word "gotta" in the phrase "someone's gotta be the horse" that put the boys instantly into a defensive and resistant position. The boys, who up to this point in the discussion have been swaggering and insulting, suddenly are reduced to being belligerent and whiny. Frank slips into the classic syntax of the little boy who attempts to refuse to let women (mothers, teachers, and girls) boss him around: "I'm not making *Black Stallion*." Clem echoes Frank's comment, but with a twist. I find Clem's statement "I'm not gonna be no black stallion" fascinating, even uncanny, because it suggests meanings that exceed our sense of what a child can or should know. On one level, Clem, like Frank, is playing the part of a little boy resisting the rule of matriarchy. According to the rules of children's argumentation, Clem's "not gonna" is linguistically the appropriate response to Shirley's "someone's gotta." Clem's words can be read as mimicking the way little boys resist little girls' attempts to make them be horses in imaginary play (I have a vague memory of a little girl persuading me to run around the playground with a jump rope in my mouth while she guided me from behind).

Whether or not he understands the full implications and resonance of his comment (it is hard to tell with Clem), he is also citing some sophisticated discourses about gender and race. In popular culture, the word *stallion* is often used (for obvious reasons) as a metaphor for hypermasculinity and male sexual prowess. The association in thoroughbred racing of stallions with being put out to stud gives the word *stallion* the meaning of a male who on the one hand lives an enviable life as the head of a harem but who, on the other hand, gets to keep his job only as long as he is able to perform sex on demand. In announcing that he refuses Shirley's directive to be a stallion in her movie, Clem thus alludes, however unintentionally, to male fantasies and anxieties about satisfying females sexually. As Clem is African American, his words also cite discourses about race that circulate in the larger society and at Koa. Clem accentuates his blackness in this statement by using a convention of Black English. "I'm not gonna be no black stallion" is not quite as black-inflected as "I ain't gonna be no black stallion," but for Clem, who speaks standard English at school (I don't know how he speaks at home), this phrasing is clearly a departure from his usual school syntax. Thus I read Clem here as citing the complaint of black actors in Hollywood who resist being limited to playing stereotypical black film parts. As it turned out, Clem's comment here anticipated a tension that would come up later in the year at Koa. When the children made their movies, typecasting became an issue in several groups, as, for example, when an unattractive girl was cast as the evil Ursula in a remake of *The Little Mermaid*.

As this interview drew to a close and it was time for the children to return to their classroom, the boys launched into an angry discussion:

FRANK: I don't want to go back.
INTERVIEWER: Why not? Don't you like school?
FRANK: Today we've got the meanest substitute.
BRANSON: I'm gonna kill her! I'm gonna kill her!
FRANK: Everyone wants to kill her.
BRANSON [to the interviewer]: Do you know what? Our reading period, Chauncy just got up to throw away a piece of rubbish and she put his name on the board.
INTERVIEWER: Maybe she's never substituted before.
FRANK: She has substituted!
BRANSON: Nah, I think just music.
CLEM: I just threw away a piece of rubbish and got sent to the office, yeah? For throwing away a piece of rubbish!

I include this postscript to the focus group discussion because it shows that even though they posture as tough males, these boys are very much under the domination of female authority, just and unjust. The reality of these boys' lives is that they spend most of their childhood under the control of women. I suggest that this may be a major factor in their performances of masculine swagger and in their tendency to belittle girls. In their dealings with girls and women, these boys are alternately swaggering and pathetic. The boys in this group, who seemed to be so much more powerful than the girls throughout the discussion, in the end seem more vulnerable and insecure than threatening. The girls said much less in the conversation, and they took a lot of grief from the boys, who were able to employ patriarchal discourses and positionalities to empower themselves vis-à-vis the girls. But this masculine power is fragile, and the boys' performances of masculine bravado are difficult to sustain.

One factor is that the power boys enjoy as males in the larger patriarchal society is mediated by the more immediately experienced matriarchal power of home and school. Another factor undermining the conviction of their macho self-presentation is that their prepubertal bodies are ridiculously unlike the bodies of the male icons with whom they attempt to identify. Watching the videotape of the focus group discussion gives a very different sense than reading the transcript because it is immediately apparent on the tape that the boys are smaller than the girls. Clem and Branson are skinny little boys. Frank is a chubby little boy. Shirley is about their size, but Jewel and Harlynn are a good deal taller and heavier than Clem and Branson. When we are aware of the smallness of their stature, their male swagger and misogyny, while still repugnant, become more pathetic, even comical, and more clearly a performance, on the order of kids dressing up as superheroes and monsters. In the end, I am left with the feeling that the boys' performances of masculinity are more desperate than the girls' of femininity because, at least at this stage of life, the parts the boys are allowed to play are more ridiculous and their chances of playing the parts convincingly more remote.

CHAPTER 4

Race

It is 11:00 A.M. on Thursday, and I've just shown a group of 7- and 8-year-old girls at Koa Elementary School the scene from *Swiss Family Robinson* in which an army of pirates attacks the Robinson family. The pirates appear to be from various Southeast Asian and Polynesian cultures. The actors playing these parts wear generic pirate bandanas, three-cornered hats, and earrings, but they also have topknots, queues, plantation-worker straw hats, and pantaloons and vests that look as if they might have been borrowed from a production of *The King and I*. The attackers carry clubs, machetes, and scimitars. The Robinson family, led by John Mills in the role of the patriarch, is White. I, too, am White. The five girls in the group of viewers are Asian American (Japanese, Chinese, and Filipino), Polynesian (Hawaiian and Samoan) or mixed. After showing this three-minute scene to the girls, I ask them a series of questions, leading up to this exchange:

INTERVIEWER: Were there good guys and bad guys?
CHILDREN [in chorus]: Yes.
INTERVIEWER: Who were the good guys?
MALIA: The ones inside the house.
LOREEN: The one who was . . . [chopping motion]
INTERVIEWER: And who were the bad people?
MALIA: The ones who were outside.
LOREEN: The ones coming up.
INTERVIEWER: How can you tell who were the good ones and who were the bad ones?
JAYLYNN: Because they were attacking.
LACEY: No, because they look, they look . . .
INTERVIEWER: 'Cause they're attacking?
LACEY: No, because they look like, they look more bad and more good.
INTERVIEWER: What makes the bad ones look bad? I don't know what you mean.
LACEY [pulling on the corners of her eyes]: Like Chinese eyes . . .

54

RACIAL INTERPELLATION

Lacey's statement is disturbing because it taps into the core of our fears and concerns about children, the media, and racism. Many of Disney's children's movies, including *Swiss Family Robinson*, contain offensive racial stereotypes, especially in the characterization of the villains. There is a danger that young children, lacking experience in making sense of the complexities of media representations of race, may be confused and misled by these stereotypes. There is cause to worry that children like Lacey, who is a member of a minority group in the larger American society, may be injured emotionally by films in which their race or ethnicity is presented in a film in a negative light. One especially pernicious form of such injury is when the minority-group child, identifying with the aggressor, is seduced by the racial semiotics of a film into seeing people who look like her as ugly or evil.

Lacey's "Chinese eyes" words and gesture are suggestive of a paradigmatic symptom of racial self-loathing and cross-race envy precipitated by popular cultural images of beauty—the eyelid operation popular among Asian American women. About half of all Japanese are born with double eyelids and half with single eyelids. With a relatively simple (though not inexpensive) surgical procedure, single eyes can be turned into double eyes. This operation is controversial in Hawai'i, as my Japanese American colleagues have explained to me. Franklin Odo, founder of the ethnic studies program at the University of Hawai'i, told me that he sometimes gets into heated discussions with his Japanese American students when he suggests that getting your eyes done constitutes a capitulation to Western standards of beauty. Lois Yamauchi, of the University of Hawai'i's College of Education, told me stories about her adolescent days in Honolulu in the 1970s, when girls with single eyes would use tape to approximate the effect of double-eyelid surgery. In *Saturday Night at the Pahala Theatre* (1993), Lois Ann Yamanaka's teenage protagonist from the Big Island of Hawai'i speaks of her desire for double eyes:

> I tell you, my next birtday
> When my madda ask me what I like,
> I going tell her I like go Honolulu
> for get one double eye operation.
> I no care if all bruise
> like Donna's one for six months.
> Look Donna now, all nice her eyes,
> and she no need buy Duo glue
> or Scotch tape anymore
> for make double eye.
> I take the operation any day. (p. 33)

Discussions of the operation are highly charged in Asian American communities because, like the Jew's nose (Gilman, 1991) and black skin (Fanon, 1963), Asian eyes function as a cultural synecdoche—the part that stands for the whole, a fetishized body part that carries such an excess of signification that mention of it produces an almost visceral feeling of discomfort.

These are among the concerns that come to mind as I reflect on Lacey's "Chinese eyes" comment. But these concerns are only speculations. What we don't know, and need to know before we go too far down the road of seeing Lacey as a victim of media racism on her way to cosmetic surgery, is what Lacey's words and gesture meant to her and to her classmates. What can Lacey's response tell us about how movies affect her understandings and experience of race? Should we read her comment as evidence that she and her classmates at Koa are susceptible to noxious racist messages in the popular culture? Or are there other ways to read her response, ways that might lead to less pessimistic conclusions?

Before attempting to answer these questions, we need to locate our concern about Lacey and her classmates within a broader understanding of the role popular media play in the formation of children's understandings of race and ethnicity. In countries where children watch a lot of television, their information about other races and cultures comes, to a significant extent, from popular media. This is especially true for children who live in communities where they have little face-to-face interaction with people unlike themselves. Where else will a child in a small town in Wisconsin encounter Arabs than in *Aladdin*, Native Americans than in *Pocahontas*, or African Americans than on sitcoms, sports telecasts, or MTV? And it is not just children's understandings about other races and cultures that are influenced by the popular media. We also have reason to be concerned about what it means to children when they see their own racial or ethnic group represented on television in stereotypical and negative ways—or rarely represented at all.

The dynamics of how the popular media contribute to children's notions of race and ethnicity are far more complex than can be explained by notions of imitation alone. We can imagine situations in which children might imitate racist behaviors they see in a film—for example, if White and Asian American children were to fight on the playground after watching *Swiss Family Robinson*. But there are more subtle and profound ways in which movies and television affect children's understandings and experience of race. Children watching *Swiss Family Robinson*, in addition to being tempted to imitate the racial warfare of the film, might come to see their own and other races from the film's point of view. In this case, they wouldn't so much imitate actions from the film as have their understandings of themselves and others transformed by the film. Such media effects are less an issue of imitation than of identification and interpellation.

What evidence do we have that Lacey and her classmates identified with the pirates or that they were interpellated by the racism of the film? Their demeanor while watching and their comments afterward make it clear that the girls paid attention to the scene. But interpellation requires more than just paying attention. Our concern about Lacey and *Swiss Family Robinson* is based on an assumption we make about a circuit of identification and internalization: Lacey, who is part Asian American, sees something of herself in the Asianness of the film's villain, who is played by a Japanese actor.

The flaw in this reasoning is that in making this assumption we are engaging in the process of racial essentializing we mean to oppose. Why do we assume that Lacey sees something of herself in the pirate and of the pirate in herself? Lacey and the pirate leader are far more different than they are similar. She is a young American girl whose maternal great-grandparents came from Japan. The pirate is a clownish character played by a middle-aged Japanese male actor in a not very realistic children's movie made 30 years ago. What do this 8-year-old girl in Pearl City and this fictional pirate have in common other than the fact that some people perceive both of them as Asian?

I don't mean to suggest that I think it preposterous or even unlikely that Lacey identifies with the villains in *Swiss Family Robinson*. What I am suggesting is that without other evidence, we cannot know and should not assume this to be the case. We underestimate the imagination of viewers and the complexity of the process of identification when we evaluate media effects by counting how many heroic and how many villainous Asian characters appear in a movie and then use this calculation to determine how the movie will affect impressionable Asian American viewers. Instead of focusing our attention on the content of media texts, we need studies of how the interpellation, identification, and internalization of media images operate in particular localities, on audiences with particular strengths and vulnerabilities.

Whether a viewer will identify with a character in a movie is a complex and not very well understood process. It is naive to assume that a viewer automatically will identify with a character who appears to be like her or won't with a character who seems to be very different. Young viewers, after all, readily identify with characters who are animals or even inanimate objects (Little Toot, for example, or the Brave Little Toaster). Film theorists and media researchers suggest that identification with characters in films often crosses gender and racial lines. Laura Mulvey (1975), writing from a psychoanalytic perspective, argues that the female film spectator may respond to the image of a beautiful woman on the screen, not by identifying with her, but by taking on the perspective of the male cinematic gaze: "For women (from childhood onwards) trans-sex identification is a habit that very easily becomes second nature" (p. 13). In *Men, Women, and Chainsaws* (1992), Clover argues that good horror films are "victim identified," as they invite male as well as female viewers to experience the fear of the victim rather than the sadism of the perpetrator. Less work has been done on ethnic than on gender issues in film and television spectatorship. Using survey data, Buckingham (1993) found that children's likes and dislikes of television characters cross racial lines. But, as Buckingham warns, liking a character is not the same thing as identifying with him.

While there are few studies of how depictions of race in films interpellate viewers, there are poignant autobiographical accounts by African Americans, Native Americans, and Asian Americans of their experiences as children with films and TV shows that presented their race either negatively or not at all. These retroactive accounts describe feelings of anger, shame, and confusion. Juliet Kono (1995) and Lois Ann Yamanaka (1996) are among the contemporary Asian American writers in Hawai'i who write poems and stories set in the past (their own and Hawai'i's) in which the Asian American child protagonist experiences a moment when she comes to realize that even if she dyes and perms her hair, she can never look like Shirley Temple or Farrah Fawcett. These memoirs suggest that images of beauty in advertising and popular culture play a key role in the formation of a racial/ethnic identity. But how, exactly, does this process work? How, and under what conditions, does the experience of watching a Shirley Temple film lead a Japanese American girl to a feeling of self-loathing and otherness? Such an outcome cannot be an effect of the film watching itself; it must be an interaction of film-watching with the sense of ethnic identity and self-worth the child is developing at home and in her community.

My hypothesis, which is a central thesis of this book, is that whether a child internalizes racist ideological messages in a film will depend largely on racial dynamics in her community. These racial dynamics are highly localized (varying from school to school) and continuously in flux (varying from one generation to the next in the same location). Consider how racial interpellation is likely to play out in three different contexts. A child who is in the racial minority in her local community (for instance, one of a handful of Asian American kids in a town in the Midwest) may be predisposed to identify with a movie character of her race because seeing someone from outside her family who has features like hers is a relatively novel and therefore salient experience. We can imagine her non-Asian classmates adding to the interpellative force of the movie by saying, "Hey, those guys in the movie have eyes like Amy's!" A minority child living in a setting such as an inner-city neighborhood where most of the people she interacts with are from her own racial group, but where the community is disempowered, fragmented, and plagued by narratives of self-blame and self-loathing, is vulnerable to internalizing negative depictions of her race in movies. This dynamic is understood by community leaders who back national pride movements, which attempt to get people to resist being interpellated by negative images from the larger culture. If, in contrast, a child is from a group that is a minority nationally but the majority in her local setting and if this group is economically, socially, and politically thriving, then I think it is less likely (but by no means impossible) that she will identify with characters in movies solely on the basis of shared racial traits.

CONTEXTUALIZING "CHINESE EYES"

Lacey and the other girls were exposed to offensive racist stereotypes in *Swiss Family Robinson*. But were they interpellated by the film? Is there evidence in the transcript that the girls identified with the film's nonwhite characters or that they came to see themselves from the perspective of the film's racist ideological horizon? To answer this question, we need to begin by reading Lacey's "Chinese eyes" response alongside the rest of the interview. This requires a careful reading of the transcript as a whole from when the *Swiss Family Robinson* tape begins.

1. Loreen: Excuse.
2. Interviewer: Can you hear?
3. Loreen: I can hear, but I can't see.
4. Interviewer: Sit down, Cassidy.
5. Cassidy: I saw this.
6. Jessica: That's a war.
7. Loreen: They're all blowing up.
8. Cassidy: I saw this already.
9. Jaylynn: Then what will happen?
10. Cassidy: I saw Part Two.
11. Malia: What is that? It's the king?
12. Cassidy [under her breath]: Nah, I never saw this. [Full voice] He's going to throw it, and the dad's going to say, "Don't throw it." Throw it, throw it please. Good, good. [Singing] Aha, good for you. Aha, aha, good for you, aha, aha, aha, aha, good for you . . .
13. Lacey: That's trampled to death. Me. Ah . . .
14. Kristie: Meow?
15. Lacey: I said, "Me. Ah."
16. Cassidy: Aha, aha, good for you . . .
17. Lacey: Did you ever watch *Snowy River*?
18. Malia: Right on his head!
19. Lacey: *The Return Back to Snowy River*?
20. Cassidy: I did.

21. Lacey: One guy got trump, tramp, tramped to death.
22. Lacey: Oh, the little kid . . .
23. Lacey: Oh, Japanese against Americans.
24. Cassidy: How long does it take?
25. Interviewer: About one more minute. Are you bored?
26. Cassidy: No.
27. Jessica: Yes.
28. Lacey: No.
29. Jessica: Yeah. I'm hungry.
30. Malia: I'm tired.
31. Cassidy: I'm getting hungry. I want to eat Cheerios now.
32. Interviewer: Okay. Watch this part.
33. Cassidy and Malia: Ha, ha, ha.
34. Lacey: They're, they're wasting wood. You should use it as paper.
35. Jaylynn: Use it as paper?
36. Lacey: Yuck.
37. Jessica: Ouch.
38. Loreen: That would hurt if that would be me.
39. Cassidy: I wouldn't do that.
40. Jaylynn: This was kind of interesting.
41. Lacey: Ow, ooh, eee. Ow, ooh, my head hurts. Ow, Bolo head man got hit.
42. Everyone [disappointed the tape has ended]: Oh!
43. Interviewer: What do you think of that movie?
44. Children: Good.
45. Loreen: We want to watch more of that movie.
46. Cassidy: It's kind of really good. Because the coconut nut is a big, big nut. If you eat too much you get very fat.
47. Lacey: That's the coconut. They call it the "coconut bomb."
48. Interviewer: Were there good guys and bad guys?
49. Children [in chorus]: Yes.
50. Interviewer: Who were the good guys?
51. Malia: The ones inside the house.
52. Loreen: The one who was . . . [chopping motion]
53. Interviewer: And who were the bad people?
54. Malia: The ones who were outside.
55. Loreen: The ones coming up.
56. Interviewer: How can you tell who were the good ones and who were the bad ones?
57. Jaylynn: Because they were attacking.
58. Lacey: No, because they look, they look . . .
59. Interviewer: 'Cause they're attacking?

60. Lacey: No, because they look like, they look more bad and more good.
61. Interviewer: What makes the bad ones look bad? I don't know what you mean.
62. Lacey [pulling on the corners of her eyes]: Like Chinese eyes, and . . .
63. Loreen [arm outstretched]: And they have knives, that's why.
64. Interviewer: So one way you could tell they were bad guys is by their eyes? Is there any other way you can tell who were the bad guys and the good guys? What made the good guys look good?
65. Jessica: Because they had clothes on that's not like junk.
66. Interviewer: They had nice clothes?
67. Cassidy [dancing in place]: Because they were so cool.
68. Loreen: 'Cuz they had clothes that, I couldn't tell 'cuz . . .
69. Interviewer: Did you feel sorry for anybody?
70. Children: No.
71. Jaylynn: Not me.
72. Interviewer: How did you feel when the coconuts were blowing up?
73. Children: Funny!
74. Interviewer: How about when the logs were hitting those guys in the head?
75. Children: Funny.
76. Interviewer: Did you feel sorry for them?
77. Children: No.
78. Jaylynn: Not me. Funny.
79. Interviewer: Why not? Isn't it sad when people get hit by logs?
80. Loreen: No, because they were bad guys.
81. Jessica: It was funny.
82. Jaylynn: Yeah. We don't like bad guys.

It doesn't work to tackle Lacey's "Chinese eyes" comment and gesture head on because the question they raise is not one of meaning but of sincerity—we know what "Chinese eyes" means, we just don't know if Lacey means it. Slavoj Zizek (1991) makes a useful distinction between clues that are hard to interpret because they are cryptic/coded and those that are hard to interpret because they are too clear. As Zizek writes of Kafka's fiction: "Its overexposed character produces a radical opacity and blocks . . . interpretation" (p. 151). I have trouble interpreting Lacey's "Chinese eyes" comment because her words, like Kafka's, carry not a lack but a surplus of meaning.

Approaching a statement out of context, there is no obvious way to know if the speaker is being parodic or sincere—sarcasm and irony are those features of speech most easily lost in translation and when speakers are quoted out of context. To discern the meaning behind Lacey's words, we need to recontextualize them. A first step toward recontextualization is to place the

"Chinese eyes" statement alongside other comments Lacey made in the session:

13. Lacey: That's trampled to death. Me. Ah . . .
17. Lacey: Did you ever watch *Snowy River*?
19. Lacey: *The Return Back to Snowy River*?
21. Lacey: One guy got trump, tramp, tramped to death.
22. Lacey: Oh, the little kid . . .
23. Lacey: Oh, Japanese against Americans.
34. Lacey: They're, they're wasting wood. You should use it as paper.
41. Lacey: Ow, ooh, eee. Ow, ooh, my head hurts. Ow, Bolo head man got hit.
47. Lacey: That's the coconut. They call it the "coconut bomb."
58. Lacey: No, because they look, they look . . .
60. Lacey: No, because they look like, they look more bad and more good.
62. Lacey [pulling on the corners of her eyes]: Like Chinese eyes, and . . .

I read these 12 statements, made in the first 2 minutes of the discussion, as evidence that Lacey, intuiting the intent of my project, decided to help me out by being as obliging an informant as possible. Just seconds after the tape starts rolling, Lacey comments on the violence in the scene ("That's trampled to death"). Her second comment, "Did you ever watch *Snowy River*?" had me baffled for a while. At first I thought she was off-topic here. But *The Man from Snowy River* (1982) and *Return to Snowy River* (1988), I eventually learned, are Australian movies featuring scenes in which the protagonists are exposed to great danger, including the threat of being trampled by stampeding horses. I think what Lacey is saying to me here is, "Oh, I get it. You are a media researcher interested in learning about how violence in movies affects young viewers. You showed us *Swiss Family Robinson* because it's a children's movie with violence in it. If I might offer a bit of constructive criticism, your choice of films is a bit dated. You might consider using a scene from one of the *Snowy River* movies next time. They have action scenes that are more realistic and disturbing."

In line 23, Lacey infers, correctly, that I am concerned not just with media representations of violence but with race as well. We can read the "Oh" in "Oh, Japanese against Americans" as "Oh, I see what you are doing. You are interested in how we will interpret a fight between Asians and Whites." Her cryptic comment "They're, they're wasting wood. You should use it as paper" suggests that she is a step ahead of me in identifying objectionable material in the film: "You are interested in the various offensive ideological messages that are contained in children's films. In addition to violence and racial tension, the clip you've shown us depicts the wanton destruction of the environment." With this comment, Lacey has accurately located (interpellated!) me as the liberal media educator, concerned about the usual litany of liberal causes: violence, sexism, racism, and the destruction of the rain forests.

Lines 41 and 47 return to the issue of violence at moments in the screening when particularly violent things happen onscreen. "Bolo head man got hit" is a pidgin expression that means, "The bald man was hit." Lines 58, 60, and 62 are Lacey's responses to my question, "How can you tell who were the good ones and who were the bad ones?" Jaylynn, in line 57, suggests that the critical difference is that bad guys attack and good guys defend. Lacey then breaks in with a tone suggesting that she feels Jaylynn isn't getting to the heart of the matter. Yes, Disney marks the bad guys as bad in many ways, including having them attack, carry violent but primitive weapons, and wear "junk" clothes. But she feels that these signifiers are less salient indicators of evil than is race. In line 60 she says that the bad guys "look more bad." When I press her to explain what she means, she spells it out, so her classmates and I (who seem a bit slow on the uptake) can understand: Disney marks the pirates as evil by giving them exaggerated Asian features. That's how these films work. This reading suggests that Lacey is less the interpellated, vulnerable victim of the film's racist ideology than a precocious critic of media (and media researcher). Her "Chinese eyes" comment then can be read as an 8-year-old's version of cultural critique. We can imagine her in 20 years giving a talk at a scholarly meeting on "Chinese Eyes: The Semiotics of Evil in Disney Films."

WRITTEN ON THE BODY

Am I too optimistic in my reading here? Up until now, I've analyzed only her words. But it is her gesture that makes her response most disturbing. Doesn't her doing, as opposed to just saying, "Chinese eyes" suggest that something other than intellectual, distanced commentary is going on here? By bringing her hands to her face, isn't she suggesting that the racism of the film has in some way touched her personally? Perhaps. But just as we must read her words carefully to discern her meaning, we need to do the same with her gesture. It is interesting that Lacey, who told me at the end of the discussion that she is Native Hawaiian and Japanese, uses the phrase "Chinese eyes" rather than "Japanese eyes." This could be read to suggest that she is not referring to herself. Similarly, we should notice that when she says "Chinese eyes," Lacey does not point to her own face. Instead, she pulls on her face, distorting its usual appearance. Her gesture, then, is not self-identifying—she uses her face as a tablet on which to produce a visual aid to support her words. Lacey is telling us that Disney uses stereotypical images of Asians, and particularly an exaggeration of the metonymic Oriental feature—single-lidded, "slanted" eyes—to signify evil. In pulling on her eyelids, I believe she is referring, then, not to the eyes of actor Sessue Hayakawa, but to the character symbolized by Hayakawa's eye makeup—purple eye shadow and black eyeliner, drawn out to his temples in a clownish version of Kabuki/ Beijing opera cosmetology. With this gesture Lacey demonstrates not an equating of herself or her own face with Oriental evil but the way she can use her fingers to make her face look ridiculous and menacing, just as Disney has done with Hayakawa's face in this movie. I read in Lacey's words and gesture an element of empathetic identification with the indignity Disney has done to Sessue Hayakawa, in turning this great bilingual actor into a grunting caricature of Oriental evil. I'm not suggesting that this is a point Lacey is making consciously or intentionally, but I nevertheless give her credit for introducing into the discussion a sense of the poignancy behind the way Hayakawa and other ethnic and especially nonwhite actors have been used by Hollywood.

For support for this interpretation that Lacey's gesture is not self-identifying, we can jump further ahead in the discussion, to another instance in which she uses her face as a tablet. After showing the children the segment from *The Black Stallion*, I queried them to see if they could correctly identify the music in the scene as having a Middle Eastern inflection:

INTERVIEWER: Was there music in that scene? What kind of music?
LACEY: It was like, umm . . . You know, like, those people [putting one finger in the center of her forehead], the people that have jewelry in their head? They dance [swinging arms] with their scarf.

Here Lacey, who is not Indian, uses her face to mime Indianness, just as she earlier used her face to mime Chineseness. In this passage, she is no more identifying herself as a bejewelled Indian dancer than she was identifying herself as an evil Oriental in the "Chinese eyes" segment. Lacey works out ideas about race and ethnicity by writing them on her body.

THEATRICALITY

The use of her face as a tablet on which to perform race is just one instance of the theatricality of Lacey's responses throughout the discussion. All speech acts are performances, but some speech contexts are more theatrical than others. The focus group interviews I conducted with the children at Koa proved to be one of these highly theatrical contexts. The videotaping of the sessions put the children in the role of television performers. Our recording setup added to the TV studio atmosphere, as the cameraperson wore earphones to monitor sound levels and checked the framing by watching a small monitor placed on a table next to the camcorder. Children periodically waved at the camera, shouted "Testing! Testing!" into the microphone, and ran around to the back of the cameraperson in an attempt to see what they looked like on the monitor. The fact that the focus group format required them to speak simultaneously to their peers and to an adult researcher heightened performativity by forcing them to be conscious of the issue of addressivity—they had to decide whether they would primarily address the researcher, their peers, or both simultaneously. The topic of our discussion—the effects of movie- and television-watching on young viewers—was another factor that contributed to the children's tendency to perform. Some children clearly were performing in order to convince me that they aren't harmed by what they watch (and thus that there is no need to censor their viewing). Bringing popular culture into the school also encouraged theatrical responses by creating a carnivalesque atmosphere—the introduction of Teenage Mutant Ninja Turtle commercials and action movies to the world of school invited the children to enact some of the pleasure they find in popular culture (Grace & Tobin, 1997).

For all these reasons, in most of the focus group discussion sessions, spirits ran high and the children were alternately giddy, shy, self-conscious, authoritative, argumentative, and naughty. The "Chinese eyes" session was performative in all these ways, and in an additional sense—Lacey, Cassidy, Jaylynn, Malia, Loreen, and Jessica performed not just individually but also as a sort of improvisational theater company. The transcript of this group's discussion reads like a playscript, with strongly drawn central characters, dramatic tension, double entendres, and surprising plot turns. We get a more complex sense of Lacey's "Chinese eyes" comment when we treat it as a line said by a character in a play and when we locate this line in the context of the dramatic action that was unfolding:

Synopsis. Act one, scene one: The houselights come up on a middle-aged man (with his back to the audience) and six little girls (facing the front of the stage) seated around a table in a school library, watching a TV monitor. We hear a film score and the sounds of explosions, gunshots, and shouts coming from the television set. Cassidy (audience right) suddenly leaps to her feet and hops around in excitement in front of the monitor. Jaylynn complains that Cassidy is blocking her view. The man, a media effects researcher, in a tone as much pleading as directing, tells Cassidy to sit down. Cassidy complies and then, in an attempt to take control of the discussion, announces, "I saw this already." Jaylynn, unconvinced, challenges Cassidy: "Then what will happen?"

Cassidy, caught in a lie and unable to predict what will happen next on the screen, tries to save face, stuttering, "I, ah, saw Part II."

Cassidy, set back but not defeated, switches tactics. Bouncing in her seat to the music of the film, she acts out the part of a highly suggestible child TV viewer who imitates and in other ways gets caught up in what she sees on the screen: "A bomb! Throw it! Good for you!" As she mimes the violence of the characters on the screen, Cassidy sneaks mischievous smiles at her friends around the table, exhorting them to loosen up and not let the school setting and the presence of an adult researcher constrain their enjoyment of the movie. Jaylynn, Malia, and Loreen (seated at the middle of the table, stage center) smile at Cassidy's antics, but they don't participate. Then, from the side of the table opposite Cassidy (stage left), Lacey speaks, as if talking to herself, but in a clear, serious voice, her words and demeanor a striking counterpoint to Cassidy's naughtiness: "That's trampled to death." Turning to the adult researcher, Lacey asks, "Did you ever watch *Snowy River?*" Lacey continues to hold the stage, bringing up appropriate concerns about the movie playing on the monitor, other violent children's movies, and the larger issue of media violence: trampling, fighting, interethnic warfare. Cassidy, unhappy that Lacey is now in control of the conversation and critical of Lacey's sucking up to the researcher with her earnest, goody-goody responses, once again changes discursive strategies, this time by trying to lead the children into a mini-insurrection: "How long does it take?" "I'm getting hungry. I want to eat Cheerios now." Lacey, interceding on the researcher's behalf, gets the conversation back on track by commenting seriously on the action on the monitor, where logs have been cut and stacked to use as a weapon against the attackers: "They're wasting wood. You should use it as paper."

The videotape ends; the monitor becomes silent; the children groan in disappointment. Cassidy once again tries to create a more festive, resistant mood with a silly comment: "the coconut nut is a big, big nut." The researcher, ignoring Cassidy's antics, perseveres with his questions: "Who were the bad guys?" First Loreen, then Jaylynn, give serious answers: The ones coming up; because they were attacking. Then Lacey, looking both at the researcher and over his shoulder at the audience (the video camera), takes command of the conversation as she earnestly explains: "No, because they look more bad . . . Like Chinese eyes." As Lacey in the left foreground of the scene pulls on her eyelids to emphasize her point, Jaylynn and Loreen, in the background, with nervous expressions on their faces, imitate her gesture. Jessica chimes in that the good guys had nice clothes. Cassidy once more tries to take control of the conversation with silliness by adding, in a singing voice, snapping her fingers, "Yeah, because they were so cool!" (End of scene).

In this opening scene, if Lacey seems familiar to us as the good girl who answers each of the teacher's questions appropriately and seriously, Cassidy is the class clown/teacher's nightmare. Cassidy persistently undermines the seriousness of the discussion, turns the discussion off-topic, and distracts the attention of the other children. Lacey and Cassidy are the play's protagonist and antagonist, with the researcher the supporting player caught in the middle of their struggle to take control of the tone and direction of the discussion, and the other children the chorus that watches and comments on the action.

But to read the dramatic tension of this scene as a power struggle between sincerity and naughtiness or between obliging the researcher versus resisting his agenda is to underestimate the complexity of this play's characters and plot. The genius of this improvised script lies in the way the audience is allowed gradually to come to understand how Lacey and Cassidy, who appear at first to be adversaries, are actually allies who use parallel tactics to resist and undermine the researcher's attempts to understand them.

To see Lacey and Cassidy only in dichotomous terms is to miss the reciprocity and underlying similarity of their responses to me. While many of the children at Koa seemed to have little or no understanding of why I was talking with them about movies, Cassidy and Lacey quickly figured me out. Lacey showed her understanding of my project by listing the litany of problematic issues in *Swiss Family Robinson* ("Japanese against Americans," "trampled to death," "wasting wood," "Chinese eyes") and by offering me advice on other movie clips I might use as cues in my subsequent research with children. Cassidy showed her understanding of my project more provocatively. Having intuited that I was showing them movie clips and television commercials for my research needs rather than for their viewing pleasure, Cassidy resisted this agenda first by encouraging the other girls to be silly ("Aha, aha, good for you") and then by telling me she was bored and hungry ("I want to eat Cheerios"). I take this comment to be a mischievous and clever reference to a segment of the research we had gone through 10 minutes earlier, in which I showed the girls a Cheerios commercial. "I want to eat Cheerios" was a way of teasing me about my research—"You're the media effects specialist who knows how commercials affect children. If you didn't want us to get hungry, you shouldn't have shown us a food commercial!"

RESISTANCE AND SOLIDARITY

Cassidy's and Lacey's understanding of my needs and desires as a researcher in turn gave them power over me: aware of what I hoped to learn from them, they were in a position either to oblige or to frustrate me. A simplistic reading of their responses would suggest that Cassidy made things difficult for me and Lacey helped me out. But it could also be argued that Cassidy, by bouncing in her chair to the movie's music, participating vicariously in the film's violence, and displaying her vulnerability to commercial appeals, actually was the one who was being obliging as she performed the part of the media researcher's suggestible, easily interpellated movie-viewing child. By being so serious in her responses, Lacey thwarted my desire to learn how watching movies affects her. By answering me not as a child viewer but as a sort of fellow researcher/media expert, Lacey hid from me other dimensions of her viewing. The indecipherability of her "Chinese eyes" comment is consistent with the way her responses throughout the interview kept me off-balance and at a distance. Both girls turned the interview into a game, performing media effects positions rather than revealing themselves to me. When we as educators or researchers succeed in getting children to say what we fear or expect them to say, we have failed, for the performative responses we elicit render the children's real feelings invisible to us. Children are adept at answering teachers' and researchers' questions in ways that make them simultaneously transparent and opaque. Cassidy and Lacey eluded my desire to see into their hearts and minds by employing opposing but in the end similar strategies: naughtiness and overcompliance.

Lacey's self-presentation as precocious media critic and compliant research subject came to a halt in the last section of the interview, when I asked the girls to analyze a segment from *The Black Stallion*. Perhaps, as far as Lacey was concerned, this was one task too many. Or perhaps she decided that she should drop the role of teacher's pet and reestablish solidarity with Cassidy and her peers in the group before leaving the interview context and heading off to lunch. Whatever her reasons, in the last few moments of the session, Lacey's resistance, which was manifested in the earlier phase of the interview in the form of overcompliance and hyperperformativity, switched to irritation, sarcasm, and even belligerence.

(The interviewer turns on the *Black Stallion* tape.)
CASSIDY: Achoo. Excuse me. [Snapping fingers] I like dance.
JAYLYNN: Go dance, then.
CASSIDY [dancing]: Do do do do. [joined by Malia]
(Tape ends)
INTERVIEWER: What did you think of that movie?
MALIA: I don't know.
CASSIDY: I want to see the whole thing.
MALIA: What was the boy doing?
CASSIDY: I need some food.
LACEY: Nothing happened.
INTERVIEWER: What did you see?
LACEY: Just a horse.
INTERVIEWER: Did that look like a good movie?

LACEY: No.

LOREEN: We'd have to see a lot.

INTERVIEWER: Would you like to see more?

CHILDREN: Yeah.

LACEY: More [exasperated, with her hands held out for emphasis], so I could learn what it is about.

CASSIDY [arms raised]: Yeah, so we could talk about it.

INTERVIEWER: Was the boy in the first shot close or far?

JESSICA: Far.

INTERVIEWER: How did that make you feel?

MALIA: We don't know.

LACEY: We don't know. We're not actress.

INTERVIEWER: When you make a movie are you gonna want to make close shots or far shots?

CHILDREN: Far shots.

INTERVIEWER: Why?

LACEY: Because we're shy. I'm shy.

INTERVIEWER: What kind of music was in that scene?

LACEY: It was like, um . . . You know, like, those people [putting one finger in the center of her forehead], the people that have jewelry in their head? They dance [swinging arms] with their scarf.

INTERVIEWER: Why do you think they used that music?

CASSIDY: Do you have a Band-Aid?

LACEY: Why?

CASSIDY: I have a cut.

Here, as in the *Swiss Family Robinson* section of the interview, Cassidy expresses her enjoyment of movies and her annoyance with my research agenda with her body: she sneezes, jumps up out of her chair, dances, and calls attention to a small abrasion on her finger. But Lacey has changed. No longer the cerebral, obliging informant, Lacey criticizes my choice of movies ("Nothing happened," "Just a horse") and attacks my research method by pointing out that by showing them only short clips rather than whole movies, I've made it difficult for them to answer my questions intelligently ("More, so I could learn what it is about"). When I ask the students to describe the camera angles, Lacey, having abandoned the role of media expert, sarcastically says, "We're not actress," by which I take it she means, "We are only children who watch movies, not actresses who appear in them, so it is ludicrous of you to ask us about production issues." I also read in her telling me that she and her friends are shy and that they are not actresses a complaint about my having videotaped the interview sessions and compelled the girls to perform.

When I asked about the film's score, Lacey returned, briefly, to her earnest response mode. But this time, in contrast to "Chinese eyes" and "jewelry in their head," Lacey not only gestured with her body—she danced, swaying to the music in her head. In dancing, Lacey shows solidarity with Cassidy, who, since the beginning of the *Swiss Family Robinson* tape, had been out of her chair, inviting the other girls to dance. In using her body to perform a show of solidarity with Cassidy, Lacey, who in the beginning of the interview seemed to be on my side, my ally in understanding children's inner thoughts and feelings, lets us know that she has changed sides or that she had only been pretending to be on my side when she played the part of the obliging and earnest informant.

ANALYZING AN APORIA

Before leaving this transcript, I want to return to a line I have already analyzed, but this time with a new, deconstructive reading. My claim that Lacey is performing the part of the concerned media critic rather than revealing her emotional reactions to the film is supported by reading "They're wasting wood, you should use it as paper" as an aporia. She says these words at the moment that John Mills, playing the father, chops through a rope with his ax, releasing a stack of logs he had arranged as a booby trap for the pirates. An aporia is a point in a spoken or written text that at first seems unproblematic but that, following Derrida, can be read deconstructively to reveal an unresolved tension or fundamental incoherence that has been patched over. Madan Sarup (1993) summarizes Derrida's approach:

> He suggests that we should fasten upon a small but telltale moment in the text which harbors the author's sleight of hand and which cannot be dismissed simply as contradiction. We should examine that passage where we can provisionally locate the moment when the text transgresses the laws it apparently sets up for itself, and thus unravel—deconstruct—the very text. (p. 43)

I had watched and read through the video transcript perhaps 50 times without noticing anything especially odd or problematic about Lacey's "wasting wood" statement. But one evening, when I shared the transcript with my qualitative research class, a student commented, "Isn't there something weird about that line about wasting wood? You aren't supposed to save trees to use them for paper. You are supposed to use less paper in order to save trees. Doesn't she have things backwards?"

Backwardness, upsidedownness, illogic, and other inversions cry out to us for deconstruction. "They're wasting wood. You should use it for paper" is inverted, as my student suggested, on several levels. It is an inversion of the usual hierarchy of humane concern: shouldn't we be more concerned for the men who are being crushed by the avalanche of logs than for the trees that are doing the crushing? It is an inversion of student and teacher roles: even before the current era of ecological consciousness, teachers have been justifying their control of the school's supply of paper by accusing students who fail to draw on the backs and to the edges of their paper of being wasteful. (Students never get to lob this accusation of wastefulness at teachers who distribute stacks of photocopied worksheets!) And it is most significantly an inversion of commonsense logic and everyday language, an inversion akin to a Freudian slip (for deconstruction owes much to psychoanalysis), which alerts us that something here, and in the text as a whole, is not what it seems. In this case, the slip reveals that Lacey is working too hard to play a part that doesn't quite hold together: a precocious media critic, concerned about media effects on children, and eager to help the visiting researcher by being as obliging as possible in her responses. If watching the clip from *Swiss Family Robinson* had actually aroused ecological concern in Lacey, she would have talked about the Robinsons' cutting down trees rather than about our need for paper. Her slip thus gives us insight into the performative dimension of her responses, insight that further supports my contention that her "Chinese eyes" response is less than or other than it seems.

RACIAL POLITICS AT KOA

I've argued that I find little evidence in the transcript to suggest that Lacey and the other girls in her group were interpellated or otherwise hurt by the racism of *Swiss Family Robinson*. But this does not mean that I think that those who make racist movies should be exonerated or that the racism in this and other films never harms children. Movies with racist images have the potential to interpellate viewers, but not all children who watch racist movies are interpellated. Again, my position in this chapter and throughout this book is to demonstrate that the meanings children make out of the movies they watch arise out of their experiences of growing up and living in a specific local context.

By a local context, I mean a particular school during a particular period of time. Children who have grown up in the Koa community in the past 10 years have had a generally positive experience of race. There are racial tensions, but on the whole I would argue that Koa is about as good as it gets in the United States in terms of a functioning multiracial community. Mixed-race friendships are very common at Koa. The children at Koa are exposed to a variety of authoritative and internally persuasive discourses on racial and ethnic differences. Lacey's ability to stand up to the interpellative force of media racism is the result of a confluence of protective factors—she is the child of a mixed-race marriage, with a Japanese American mother and a Native Hawaiian father. She seems to be a well-adjusted, happy student in a school that has a mixture of East Asian, Southeast Asian, Polynesian, White, and Black students. Her teachers and community leaders are for the most part Asian American or Hawaiian, so she has no lack of positive role models, and no reason in her local context to perceive of her Asianness or Hawaiianness as being odd, embarrassing, or problematic. Koa is a community where local discourses about race and experiences with people of various racial backgrounds give children a good foundation from which to resist the racism of globally circulating media productions.

The tensions that exist in the larger Hawaiian political and social context among Japanese Americans, Native Hawaiians, and Whites at times are felt at Koa. But because these three groups at this particular time are relatively equal in power and influence within the Koa community, racial stereotyping and teasing are in check. The White kids occasionally get teased as *haole* newcomers, but this is balanced by the fact that Whites are the majority group in the larger national context and by their economic, social, and political success in Hawai'i. The Japanese American kids at Koa, many of whom are the grandchildren of plantation workers, are growing up in a era when Japanese American children in Hawai'i, most of whom are middle-class, are much less likely to feel different and marginalized than their counterparts did in the 1950s, 1960s, and 1970s, as described by Yamanaka, Kono, and other local writers. Native Hawaiians still face daunting social and economic problems, but it is an exciting time to be young and Hawaiian. The sovereignty movement, the Hawaiian cultural renaissance, and the development of Hawaiian-language immersion programs at Koa and elsewhere in the state (Yamauchi, Ceppi, & Lau-Smith, 1999) have given the Hawaiian children at Koa a sense of cultural identity and pride they didn't have just a decade ago. In contrast, because they are fewer in number and newer to Hawai'i, Samoans, Filipinos, and, particularly, African Americans are the groups at Koa that are most likely to be victims of racism and stereotyping.

Because a majority of the people they deal with in their everyday life are Asian, Polynesian, or a mixture of the two, the children at Koa are unlikely to associate caricatures of Asians and Polynesians in a film with actual Asians and Polynesians. My hunch is that for most children at Koa, the Japanese pirate character in *Swiss Family Robinson* is no more like a real Asian than Snoopy is like a real dog. The children might refer to Snoopy as a dog, but their experience of watching Snoopy on television doesn't change their understanding of what actual dogs are like. Similarly, for most of the children at Koa, the behavior of the Asian and Polynesian pirates in *Swiss Family Robinson* may affect their understanding of what it means to be a pirate, but it is unlikely to have much influence on the way they think about what it means to be Asian or Polynesian.

I say for "most" rather than for "all" of the children at Koa because there are some exceptions. For example, Michael (whom we met in Chapter 2) is a military dependent who had been living in Hawai'i for only a year at the time of the discussions. Having grown up on and around military bases on the U.S. mainland, Michael had an understanding of Asians and Polynesians very different from that of his classmates who grew up in the Koa community. We can see this difference in the first comment Michael made in the interview when watching the tape: "Oh, Japanese pirates. They look like the guys who mow our lawn." For those of us who live in Hawai'i, Michael's observation here is not hard to interpret. Many people in Hawai'i employ crews of gardeners, and many of these laborers are Filipino, Samoan, and Tongan. We can imagine how their arrival at his house would have looked to Michael the first time he saw them from his living room window:

> An old pickup truck rolls up Michael's driveway. Out of the back come six Polynesian and Filipino men. Some wear woven hats, others bandanas. Their clothes are tattered and dirty. One is shirtless. Another is dressed in a *lava-lava* (wraparound skirt). They are carrying shovels, picks, weed wackers, and machetes. Grim expressions on their faces, they fan out across Michael's yard.

We can see how the arrival of the gardening crew would have reminded Michael of a scene from *Swiss Family Robinson* and vice versa.

I suggest that Michael is easily interpellated by this movie's racism where most of the other children at Koa are not because he is its intended audience, the audience the movie is best able to address. The movie's plot, like those of the eighteenth- and nineteenth-century novels on which it was based (Daniel Defoe's *Robinson Crusoe* and Johann David Wyss's *Swiss Family Robinson*), is about contrast and conflict between civilized Whites and primitive people of color. In each of these versions of the story, the crucial action scene involves the White protagonist(s) successfully repelling the attack of savages. The Whites employ self-control, planning, and technological sophistication to defend their island home from rampaging dark-skinned people wielding knives and clubs. This 250-year-old storyline still works unproblematically for many viewers today because in many areas of the world White people still locate themselves within the story's ideological framework. Many White people subjectively experience the world as one in which they are the blameless potential victims of irrational violence from dark-skinned people. This story, of good, decent White folks moving to an unsettled land, making a nice home, and then being attacked by savages, is used in movies set in

India (*Gunga Din*), Africa (*Zulu*), and North America (*Fort Apache*); in political campaigns (e.g., George Bush's Willie Horton spot); and in news stories (including cases in the 1990s in Massachusetts and South Carolina in which a middle-class White person murdered a member of his or her family and then told the police and a credulous public that the crime was committed by a Black assailant). In Honolulu, violent attacks by nonwhites on Whites are relatively rare. But living in a setting where White people are in the minority is subjectively experienced by some White newcomers as a source of disempowerment, alienation, and endangerment.

Although Michael's comment that the pirates remind him of his family's gardeners was insensitive, I don't think his words were harmful or hurtful in this particular local context. They seem more provocative when I read them in the transcript than they do when I go back to the videotape of his focus group discussion. As I watch the tape, I see a small, insecure White kid sitting at a table with five more self-assured local kids. As the pirate attack on the Robinsons plays on the monitor, Michael appears nervous, even worried, while the other boys laugh and cheer. Michael's comment about gardeners is directed neither to his peers nor to me—he mumbles these words as if he were talking to himself, struggling to make sense both of the action on the screen and of race relations in Hawai'i. If the other boys heard his comment, they chose to ignore it, as they ignore or make fun of other comments Michael makes throughout the discussion. For instance, later in the discussion, Michael brags about having a Sega Genesis and a Nintendo. Jared sarcastically replies, "That's because you're rich." Brayson adds, "You lucky!" Attempting to recover from the faux pas of presenting himself as more privileged than his peers, Michael replies in a pleading voice to Jared, "But you said you have one, too." Jared replies, "No, I didn't. You lie, you Portagee." "Portagee" is an ironic, complex signifier when used in this context. The Portuguese in Hawai'i are the butt of local jokes in which they are presented as being stupid and dense. But the Portuguese generally are well-liked by other ethnic groups. The Portuguese, who came to Hawai'i as sailors and plantation foremen, were neither labor nor management. This intermediate, anomalous position in Hawaiian colonial history continues to give Portuguese Americans an anomalous position in contemporary Hawai'i as Caucasians who aren't *haoles*. Thus, in calling Michael a "Portagee," Jared is using a local expression that functions to emphasize his and the other local kids' privileged insider status in the discussion and more generally at Koa. But there is also something magnanimous about Jared's insult, for by calling Michael "a Portagee," he is suggesting that Michael should be a recipient of the group's indulgence as well as laughter. (At Koa, it is much better for a White kid to be called a Portagee than a "stupid fuckin' *haole*.") Again, the point I want to emphasize is the importance of context in the politics of ethnicity and race. In many other places in the United States, and even in many other local settings in Hawai'i, Michael's comments would be more hurtful and harmful. But in this particular conversation, in the particular local setting of Koa, to be a *haole* is to be odd and vulnerable, and to be Asian or Polynesian is to be normal and empowered.

POSTSCRIPT

I've often been asked why I didn't go back and ask Lacey what she meant by her "Chinese eyes" words and gesture. In fact, I did. I repeated the focus group interviews with all the children at Koa in the spring, 6 months after the initial interviews. The second time around, when I asked the girls how they could tell who were the bad guys, Lacey answered, "They have Japanese eyes."

I argued earlier in this chapter that it was significant that Lacey in the original interview said "Chinese eyes" rather than "Japanese eyes," because this made it less likely that she was referring to herself. What, then, do we make of her saying "Japanese eyes" six months later? The problem with returning to one's informants for clarification of earlier statements is that this is as likely to open up new questions as to resolve old ones. Going back for clarification is based on several questionable assumptions: that informants know why they said what they said; that they can figure out retrospectively what their words in an earlier conversation meant; and that they will be more direct and revealing in a follow-up interview than they were the first time around. My experience reinterviewing the "Chinese eyes" group suggests that these assumptions are not always true.

To follow this group longitudinally, I showed them the *Swiss Family Robinson* tape and had a discussion with them each year until they graduated from Koa. The girls said many interesting things in each of these interviews, but nothing they said explains their statements in the original interview. Each year, when we repeated the interview, the girls would beg me to show them the videotape of their discussion from the first year, the original "Chinese eyes" tape. With each passing year, when the tape began to roll, Cassidy would be more embarrassed by her exuberance and naughtiness as an 8-year-old. All the girls were struck by how much they had grown up. When the moment came on the tape where Lacey does her Chinese eyes gesture, the girls would laugh (at Lacey, at themselves, at me, with me?) and pull on the corners of their eyes. Each year, I asked Lacey what she had meant by the remark she made back in the fall of second grade, when she was 8. She never would or could tell me exactly. The closest she came was the third time we repeated the exercise, when she was 10 years old:

INTERVIEWER: Do you want to see what you said the first time? Tell me if you still agree with what you said. [rolls tape]

CASSIDY: Oh, why am I doing that? [covers face and giggles]

INTERVIEWER: Lacey, do you know why you said that about *Snowy River*?

LACEY: I don't know.

INTERVIEWER: What reminded you of *Snowy River*?

LACEY: Oh, the logs, and stuff like that.

LACEY: Look! We're saying things that we're not supposed to say, Cassidy.

CASSIDY: No, I didn't!

LACEY: You said "I'm hungry!"

CASSIDY: I didn't hear what I said.

INTERVIEWER: You said "I want to eat Cheerios!"

CASSIDY: I didn't say that!

LACEY: You did!

INTERVIEWER: Are you embarrassed when you see this?

CASSIDY: Yes!

JAYLYNN: I look like I'm a little kid!

LACEY: You look so cute, Jaylynn—you can see your little panty outline!

INTERVIEWER: When Cassidy said that about Cheerios, I think she was teasing me. I think you were saying, "If you show me a commercial about Cheerios, it makes me want to eat Cheerios." What do you think?

[Cassidy holds her arms out and shrugs]

INTERVIEWER: Maybe?

CASSIDY: Yeah. No. I don't know.

INTERVIEWER: Lacey, why did you say "They're wasting wood"?

LACEY: Cause they're [mimes chopping wood]

INTERVIEWER: What about when I ask you "What makes the bad guys look bad?"

LACEY: Chinese eyes! They make whatever the bad guys are Chinese.

INTERVIEWER: What do you mean by that?

LACEY: Because of evil eyes. [pulls up on her eyes with all ten fingers]

INTERVIEWER: Who had evil eyes?

JAYLYNN [pulling on her eyes]: Meeee!

LACEY: The bad guys, and . . .

INTERVIEWER: All the bad guys?

LACEY: Well, some had Japanese hats.

LOREEN: Lacey's talking like a baby again.

MALIA: That's how she talks when the camera's on.

INTERVIEWER: So what do you mean by saying the bad guys have Chinese eyes, Lacey? That all Chinese people are bad?

LACEY: Yeah, they have evil eyes, that go like that. [pulling on her eyes]

INTERVIEWER: But in real life, is it like that?

LACEY: No. It's animation movie, camera movie.

INTERVIEWER: Some people are worried that when they hear you talk about people with Chinese eyes or Japanese eyes that, well . . . Some of you are part-Chinese or part-Japanese, right? Tell me again what you are.

LACEY: I'm Japanese, and lots of things, but I don't know all of them. I have lots, I don't know, Japanese, Hawaiian, Chinese, some other things.

CASSIDY: Half-Filipino, half-Hawaiian.

JESSICA [in a singsong voice, pulling her eyes toward her temples]: My mommy is Chinese. [pulling her eyes toward her earlobes] My daddy is Japanese. [pulling one eye up and one down] And I'm all mixed up!

[everyone laughs and repeats Jessica's final gesture]

LOREEN: Oh yeah. [singing, joined by the other girls, who all pull their eyes toward their temples] Japanese! [pulling their eyes toward their earlobes] Chinese! [pulling in various directions] Olo-olo. [Pushing their faces in with their palms] Squash!

INTERVIEWER: What's "Olo-olo?"

LOREEN: I don't know.

MALIA: Like all crazy mixed up.

INTERVIEWER: Is that how Japanese and Chinese people's eyes go? Chinese go up and Japanese go down?

CASSIDY: Yeah.

LOREEN: We're just joking.

MALIA [to Interviewer]: What are you?

CASSIDY: Duh, he's *haole*. Can't you tell?

INTERVIEWER: Yeah, I'm a *haole*. But there's different kinds of *haoles*. I'm Jewish.

MALIA: What's Jewish?

LACEY: Like that thing they say. Shalom. And [touching the top of her head] they wear that little hat.

INTERVIEWER: Right. But I want to go back to what I was asking you about before because I really want to understand this. Lacey, you just said that you're part-Chinese and you said before that the bad guys have Chinese eyes. Should we be worried about that?

LACEY: No, they're more longer Chinese than me, even though I have Chinese eyes.

INTERVIEWER: They used makeup to make their eyes look funny, didn't they?

LACEY: Yeah, they used some kind of glue to hold it back. But how can they see when their eyes are like that? [pulling hard on her eyes and squinting] It's a little blurry.

Yes, it definitely is a little blurry. Going back to Lacey and the other girls for explanations of their earlier statements only gives me more cryptic material to analyze. I think Lacey most adequately explains what she meant by "Chinese eyes" when she says, "They're more longer Chinese than me, even though I have Chinese eyes." I take this to mean that she acknowledges that she, like Hayakawa, has single-lidded eyes, but that the pirate character in the movie is unlike Lacey and other actual Asians in that his eyes have been artificially narrowed by the use of makeup. Here, as in the original transcript, Lacey doesn't hesitate to use her own face as a canvas on which to perform racial stereotypes. She even mimes wearing a yarmulke. Her substitution, in the second interview, of "Japanese eyes" for "Chinese eyes" reveals the fluidity of her notions of race and ethnicity, a fluidity reflected as well in the silly songs the girls sing in the fourth interview, in which they perform a series of ethnicities simply by changing the angle at which they pull their eyes. When I asked Lacey directly if she believed that in real life "Chinese eyes" were characteristic of evil, she assured me that she knows *Swiss Family Robinson* is only a movie. When she says "animation movie" and "camera movie," I take it that Lacey is pointing to the movie's lack of realism. I find these comments, reassuring as they seem to support my earlier hunch that Lacey has not been interpellated by the racism of the movie. But going back to Lacey for clarification and reassurance accomplishes little in the end. Her repetition of her "Chinese eyes" words and gesture each time I show her the *Swiss Family Robinson* tape only compounds the uncanniness and sense of uninterpretable performativity of the original interview.

I do not mean to suggest that as researchers we can never benefit by doing follow-up interviews. I can think of many examples of psychotherapists and sociolinguistic researchers who, by working with the same child over time and engaging in repeated one-on-one interviews, develop deep understanding and offer convincing interpretations of children's words and actions. Examples include the clinical case studies of Erik Erikson (1964) and Bruno Bettelheim (1972); Cindy Dell Clark's (1995) investigations into children's belief in Santa Claus, the Tooth Fairy, and the Easter Bunny; Peggy Miller's (Miller et. al, 1993) analysis of her three-year-old son's evolving engagement with the Peter Rabbit story; and Jean Briggs's (1998) case study of a young Inuit boy's emotional development.

Such intrapsychic analyses are one way to make sense of a child's utterance. But there are other ways. I have chosen to focus on the social rather than intrapsychic world of the children at Koa. I didn't have and didn't seek the kind of dyadic closeness with the children at Koa that would have offered me the kind of access to their psyches that Erikson and Bettelheim had as therapists, Briggs as an ethnographic resident in an Inuit village, Clark as a childlike interviewer, and Miller in her dual role as a parent/researcher. Instead, I have restricted myself to making sense of the conversations I had access to in my role at Koa as a media researcher and educator.

Had I engaged with Lacey in more contexts, talking to her one-on-one, observing her in the classroom, on the playground, and at home, and interviewing her parents, I no doubt could have developed a deeper understanding of what she meant by "Chinese eyes." A case study of Lacey over time and across contexts would have allowed me to more confidently read the feelings and intentions behind her words and to understand how the images in *Swiss Family Robinson* connect with hundreds of other experiences and images to forge her beliefs about race and her sense of ethnic identity. But such an in-depth analysis of an individual isn't the goal of my project.

Instead, I find it more meaningful to heed Voloshinov's advice to read the ambiguous and ambivalent utterances of an individual as reflections of social rather than intrapsychic tensions and dynamics. Following Voloshinov's argument that the tensions and contradictions of a stratified, heterogeneous society inevitably will be manifested in the words of its individual citizens, I read the ambiguous and sometimes contradictory statements about race and culture offered by Lacey and her classmates as expressions of the tensions and contradictions that surround race in both their local community and the larger society. Viewing and discussing the *Swiss Family Robinson* clip was an occasion for Lacey and her classmates to engage with both global and local discourses on race. They know that race matters in globally circulating media texts where being White is the most privileged and natural thing to be, the *unmarked* racial category (Phelan, 1993), and where being Asian is problematic—a hodgepodge of stereotypes, including dragon lady, warlord, camera-toting tourist, science nerd, martial arts specialist, and loyal sidekick. The children know that race matters in the state of Hawai'i, where White, Asian American, and Polynesian groups vie for economic, political, and cultural power. And they know that race matters locally, at Koa, where being Asian American is the most normal thing to be. The conversations I held with the children at Koa are sites where these global, regional, and local discourses were verbalized, circulated, re-accented, and given new meaning.

CHAPTER 5

Colonialism

Four Koa second-graders discuss *Swiss Family Robinson*:

INTERVIEWER: Was that a commercial?
MARY-JEAN: No. It was a movie.
INTERVIEWER: How could you tell?
NOLAN: It was longer.
DEREK: And, um, the Indians lost.
INTERVIEWER: Who were the good guys in that movie?
NOLAN: The ones that was winning.
MARY-JEAN: The ones with the coconut bombs.
INTERVIEWER: Were there any bad guys in the movie?
DEREK: Yeah. The Indians.
INTERVIEWER: How could you tell they were bad?
NOLAN: Because they tried to kill them.
DEREK: Yeah, they were trying to attack.
INTERVIEWER: Is there a difference between the way the good guys and the
    bad guys look?
MARY-JEAN: No.
DEREK: Yeah. Because one was the Indians and one was the Americans.
INTERVIEWER: Which were the good ones?
NOLAN: Americans.
INTERVIEWER: Which were the bad ones?
DEREK: Indians.
INTERVIEWER: Anything else on how they looked?
NOLAN: Yeah. The Indians has knives and stuff.
INTERVIEWER: Is that how Indians are?
NOLAN: Yeah.
DEREK: And good guys have tricks and bombs.
INTERVIEWER: Do they look different?
DEREK: Yeah, one looked mean and one didn't.
INTERVIEWER: Did you see any girls in this? Were the girls good or bad?

MARY-JEAN: Good.
INTERVIEWER: Did you see any girls that were with the bad guys?
DEREK: No.
INTERVIEWER: Why do you suppose that is?
NOLAN: Cuz Indians don't have girls.
HISAE: I saw some girls.
MARY-JEAN: Yes, they have girls. Only some.
NOLAN: Only the boy Indians fight when they go out.
INTERVIEWER: What do you think the girls were doing?
DEREK: Staying home.
NOLAN: Taking care of babies.

Something is wrong here, wrong in the sense of "strange" or "awry." I am saying "Something is wrong here" the way a detective at the scene of a crime might say, "Something's fishy. Something doesn't add up." I'm not referring to the idea that the girl Indians stay home taking care of babies. That idea is wrong in the sense of being sexist, but, unfortunately, it's not strange or hard to explain. What is strange, what needs explaining, what doesn't add up, is how Indians got into this conversation in the first place. *Swiss Family Robinson* takes place on an unnamed tropical island in the middle of an unnamed ocean. The bad guys in the film are played by Asian and Polynesian actors costumed as pirates. Why, then, do Derek and Nolan refer to these pirates as Indians? Is this a case of mistaken identity?

You may be thinking that the boys meant Indians in the sense of people from the Indian subcontinent. A reasonable enough surmise, but I don't think it is the right explanation. For one thing, the pirates aren't costumed to look Sikh, Bengali, or Hindi—they look as though they could be from Malaysia or the Philippines, but not from India. And children in Hawai'i rarely use the word Indian to mean South Asian; they almost always use it to mean Native American. American Indians make frequent appearances in the Hawai'i elementary school social studies curriculum, especially around Thanksgiving. India, in contrast, is absent year-round. And in contrast to the paucity of South Asian characters and settings in the American popular media, American Indians are featured characters in many children's books, movies, and television shows. For these reasons, most children in Hawai'i know next to nothing and care relatively little about India, but they know a lot and think a lot about American Indians. What I find disturbing about Derek's and Nolan's mistakes is that I fear it is what they know and think about Native Americans that leads them to call the bad guys in the movies Indians. What makes me cringe is the thought that these children are using the word *Indian* here as a metonym for men who are dark-skinned, dangerous, stupid, and uncivilized.

This mistake is even more disturbing in view of the fact that these two boys were not the only children at Koa who made it. In 6 of the 32 focus groups in this study, children said that the bad guys in *Swiss Family Robinson* were Indians. And all these groups were made up of second-, third-, or fourth-graders (that's half of the 12 groups in this age range). We have a mystery to solve: Why do so many of Koa's 7-, 8-, and 9-year-olds misidentify the pirates in *Swiss Family Robinson* as Indians?

Looking at the transcripts from the focus group discussions in which the pirates were called Indians, we find a pattern emerging—whenever the word *Indian* appears, it is in the company of comments about bad guys with mean faces who don't have nice clothes, houses, or families. We can get a better sense of how these elements came together in the discussions by considering extended extracts from two more transcripts. First, a mixed group of third-grade boys and girls:

INTERVIEWER: Who were the good guys?
AMBER: The ones throwing the coconut bombs and the logs.
INTERVIEWER: Who were the bad guys?
KASIA: The people who were throwing the bombs. So they could die.
MITCHELL: No. I think the good guys were the ones throwing the bombs, 'cause the bad guys they, good people, they don't get Indians and all these people to kill them.
INTERVIEWER: Were those Indians?
MITCHELL: Yeah.
KASIA: They had funny hair, they dressed funny, and they had mean faces.
AMBER: If the bad guys were the ones throwing bombs, they wouldn't have little kids with them.
INTERVIEWER: Was it a true story?
WILLIAM: Maybe, it could be.
INTERVIEWER: Could it happen in Hawai'i?
MITCHELL: Yeah, they could take boats to here, and they could have a fight with us.
INTERVIEWER: Did you feel sorry for anyone?
KASIA: No. 'Cause the bad guys were trying to kill them, so they try to protect themselves.
AMBER: I felt sorry for the good guys, 'cause they were getting attacked.

And a combined group of third- and fourth-grade girls:

STEPHANIE: That's, um, I think, Indians and cowboys.
DESIREE: Oh, those are pirates and Indian cowboys.
ASHLEY: Oh, I saw this!

AMANDA: Me, too! You remember the boy, he dropped coconuts on the pirate's head.

ASHLEY: He got hit in the head.

STEPHANIE: Those would hurt!

DESIREE: Oh! I don't want that!

INTERVIEWER: Okay, what did you think about that?

AMANDA: It was a killing and war movie.

ASHLEY: It's a war movie.

INTERVIEWER: Do you think that could really happen?

DESIREE: Yeah.

ASHLEY: I think so.

INTERVIEWER: Could it happen in Hawai'i?

AMANDA: Maybe at the sea or something.

STEPHANIE: No.

INTERVIEWER: You don't think that could happen in Hawai'i?

STEPHANIE: People here are too nice.

INTERVIEWER: Were there good guys in this? Who were the good guys?

AMANDA: The ones that were throwing the coconut.

INTERVIEWER: What did the good guys look like?

AMANDA: White shirts.

DESIREE: A girl wearing a black dress and the boys wearing long pants and a t-shirt.

INTERVIEWER: What did the bad guys look like?

ASHLEY: They're pirates.

AMANDA: Some had swords.

INTERVIEWER: How could you tell they were the bad guys and the other guys were good?

STEPHANIE: I think they were both bad, because they were both throwing at each other and stuff and they didn't try to stop it or anything.

DESIREE: I think the Indians were bad.

ASHLEY: I think they're good guys, 'cause usually good guys don't charge.

AMANDA: Yeah, 'cause the bad guys charged with swords and stuff.

STEPHANIE: It's hard to explain, but usually I can tell the bad guys. Usually the bad guys have more men, and the good guys have less.

INTERVIEWER: How did they make the bad guys and the good guys look different?

ASHLEY: They made them different colors and made them have different kinds of weapons.

INTERVIEWER: How did they make them different colors?

DESIREE: Oh, I know why they made them look like bad guys and good guys, because they were charging each other, one team was on one side, and the other team . . .

ASHLEY: One side could have been good guys and one of them could have
    been bad guys.
INTERVIEWER: Do you think pirates really look like that?
ASHLEY: Sometimes.
AMANDA: I don't think so. I think the bad guys should all wear one of
    those red belts, like Jennifer's, like a red string, and a white shirt and
    black pants.
INTERVIEWER: Did you see any girls in this movie?
STEPHANIE: One. She had a blue dress.
INTERVIEWER: Was she good or bad?
STEPHANIE: Good.
INTERVIEWER: How could you tell?
STEPHANIE: She had a dress on, and the girls wouldn't be wearing a dress if
    she was bad.
ASHLEY: They wear pants.
INTERVIEWER: There weren't any girl pirates? I wonder why.
ASHLEY: 'Cause men are more stronger than girls.
INTERVIEWER: Did you feel sorry for anybody?
STEPHANIE: No.
INTERVIEWER: What about when the logs were rolling down on them?
DESIREE: It was funny.
STEPHANIE: Because they were so mean.
DESIREE: They were trying to kill the others so the other people got to kill
    them.

THE TEXTUAL INSIGHTS OF YOUNG CHILDREN

Because we are adults and Derek, Mitchell, Desiree, and the other informants
quoted above are children, the question "Why do these children call the pirates in *Swiss Family Robinson* Indians?" inevitably carries the implication
"Why do these children make *the mistake* of calling the pirates in *Swiss Family Robinson* Indians?" But what if we were to approach the problem differently, this time with the assumption that the statement "The bad guys are
Indians" is not a mistake but an insight? The question then becomes: What
are these children seeing that we don't see that leads them to call the pirates
Indians?

    Before attempting to answer this question, let me first clarify one of
the implications of my argument. It would be reasonable to assume that as
children grow up they develop increasingly sophisticated understandings of
movies. Such developmental narratives are the way we tend to understand

children's sexual, cognitive, moral, and psychosocial development. Why shouldn't a similar progression be true of how children watch and understand films? But what I'm suggesting here is not a developmental argument. Instead, I'm offering the idea that children of a certain age may have understandings of movies that are not just different from but in some ways better than those of older children and adults. There may be something children come to know about the world and the media at ages 7 or 8 that they lose when they get a bit older.

I can clarify my point by giving an example of what I am not talking about. When my sons were preschool-age they found nothing wrong with the idea of mixing toys of different genres in their fantasy play. They would set up battles in which a combined force of G.I. Joes, transforming robots, and cowboys on horseback fought against Skeletor, Fisher-Price pirates, and Darth Vader. To my sons at this age, the larger narratives in which these toys were located (outer space, mythology, World War II, the American West) didn't much matter. But at age 5 or so they entered a stage when rigid genre distinctions came into their play. I would bring them a bucket of toys to play with in the bath and be lectured: "No, Dad, that's wrong. Pirates don't go with *Star Wars*. You can't mix them!"

When I first heard the children at Koa referring to the pirates in *Swiss Family Robinson* as Indians, I assumed that they were making the sort of mistake my sons made as 3-year-olds when they ignored the genre of their toys in their fantasy battles. But the children who called the pirates Indians in the focus group interviews were 7- and 8-year-olds, well beyond preschool age. Were these children, then, developmentally slow in their media-watching? No, what I suspect is going on here is that the children who call pirates Indians are finding meaning in the text that eludes most younger and older children as well as adults. Unlike younger children, these 7- and 8-year-olds are very clear about the difference between Indians and pirates, and they know full well that Indians don't belong in pirate movies. Therefore, what I think these children are saying is, "This is not, at heart, a pirate movie. It is an Indians and settlers movie!" I am suggesting that the children who call the pirates Indians are making intertextual connections between the *Swiss Family Robinson* scene I showed them and cowboys-and-Indians movies they have watched. They are reading the film's latent rather than manifest plot. They are saying, in effect,

> This movie is set on a tropical island, the bad guys are dressed as pirates, and the good guys are supposedly Swiss (at least they're referred to as a Swiss family in the film's title, and the sons are named Ernst and Fritz). But the staging of the big action scene is right out of a Hol-

lywood Western. Take away the pirate costumes, kabuki makeup, and tropical setting, and you've got a traditional Hollywood version of White settlers being attacked by marauding Indians.

If this is what the children are getting at when they call the pirates Indians, I think they are dead right about this movie and, more generally, about the interchangeability of ethnic bad guys in action films.

If anyone is mistaken here, it is we adults and the older children who call the pirates in *Swiss Family Robinson* pirates even though these villains don't behave at all as pirates typically do in movies. Almost all the action in the film takes place on land. The pirates are nonwhite. Unlike movie pirates, these bad guys don't use flintlock pistols or cutlasses when they attack, and they aren't cunning. Instead, they attack in the classic style of Hollywood Indians and African tribesmen: with primitive weapons, they charge the good guys' well-defended fortress, running directly into enemy fire. The only strengths they bring to the battle are their bloodthirstiness and their overwhelming numerical advantage.

The best way I can think of to convince you that the pirates in *Swiss Family Robinson* are indeed acting like Hollywood Indians is to recommend that you rent the film for yourself. As you watch the battle scene, translate the "Pirate Chief" (as he's listed in the credits) into the chief of an Apache war party in a Hollywood Western, the army of pirates into braves on the warpath, and the Robinson family into White settlers fighting from behind a circle of covered wagons and see if the scene doesn't make more sense.

I suggest that this similarity between *Swiss Family Robinson* and a western is no accident. In "Ambush at Kamikaze Pass," Tom Engelhardt (1987) argues that Hollywood movies featuring White people battling Asian, African, or Polynesian natives draw heavily on the storyline and conventions of the western:

> Just as the style and substance of the Indian wars was a prototype for many later American intrusions into the Third World (particularly the campaigns in the Philippines and Indochina), so movies about those wars provide the prototype from which nearly every American movie about the Third World derived.... These Third World movies are pale reflections of the framework, outlook, and even conventions of the cowboy movie. (p. 482)

Swiss Family Robinson is a perfect example of a Third World movie that reflects the framework, outlook, and conventions of the western. The Robinsons are the good guys because they are a patriarch-led nuclear family who are industrious, clean, nicely dressed, and technologically sophisticated and who transform nature, raise crops, domesticate animals, and build, maintain, and cleverly furnish an attractive, efficient house.

The 7- and 8-year-old children who called the pirates Indians thus can be seen as having correctly identified *Swiss Family Robinson* as belonging to the genre of Hollywood films that presents the moral superiority of White settlers in colonial settings as the natural order of things. Like Engelhardt and other sophisticated cultural critics, these children are reading the deep structure of the film rather than just the manifest meaning. My hunch is that around the age of 8 or 9, children become less intuitive and spontaneous in their thinking and talking about movies as they learn to see and talk about the world in more conventional terms. These older children might notice on some level that the pirates are acting like Indians, but since this insight is counterintuitive and unconventional, they tend to repress it rather than express it in group conversation.

Learning how to watch movies is as much a process of learning what to screen out or repress as what to notice. By age 10 or so, the children at Koa have learned that no matter how else a character looks or behaves, if he flies the skull and crossbones from his mast and has a cutlass and a gold earring, he's a pirate. As they watch the film clip from *Swiss Family Robinson*, these older children have learned to push out of their thoughts all clues to the contrary in order to be able to provide a socially conventional reading of the heroes and villains in the movie. The ability and inclination to read beneath the surface narrative to the deep structure of movies may reappear in adolescence or adulthood, especially in film buffs and academicians. But for older children and most adults, interpretation of the meaning beneath the surface is bracketed and kept an arm's length away, as a second or other way of seeing and understanding. Where a 7-year-old might say of *Swiss Family Robinson*, "the pirates *are* Indians," the adolescent or adult interpreter of this movie is more likely to display awareness of both deep and surface structures by saying, "The pirate characters in the movie have been made to act like Hollywood Indians." The interpretation is more or less the same, but the pre-latency-age child's mode of reading and talking about the text is more immediate and visceral.

WHAT CHILDREN DO WITH STEREOTYPES

I have provided an answer to the question that I raised earlier in this chapter—the children who call the pirates in *Swiss Family Robinson* Indians do so because they are reading intertextually, at the level of deep rather than surface meaning. But in the course of solving this mystery, I have opened up several others. The three transcripts I've presented in this chapter are full of worrisome statements. I ask the children how they tell the good guys from the bad guys in *Swiss Family Robinson*, and they respond with normative statements linking goodness and badness to race, class, and gender. Like Lacey's "Chinese eyes" statement, this presents us with the challenge of figuring out whether my respondents are just describing how the film works or endorsing the film's racist, colonialist, and sexist ideological positions. To borrow a phrase from Julian Sefton-Green (1990), is what we are seeing here an example of what stereotypes do with children or what children do with stereotypes?

If we are to have any hope of answering these questions, we need to sort out three interrelated concerns: the children's cinematic literacy (their ability to "read" the movie), their participation in the movie's pleasures, and their vulnerability to the movie's ideological messages. It is important to remember (as most media researchers do not) that these are three different things. A child, for example, might or might not read the pirates in *Swiss Family Robinson* as generic Hollywood savages; she might or might not participate in the pleasure the film offers viewers who can set aside any concerns they have about racism, colonialism, and heteronormativity and enjoy a movie that shows White men, with the assistance of White women, blowing up and chopping down Asians and Polynesians; and she might or might not accept the film's ideological version of the world as applying to real life. For instance, when a Native Hawaiian child states, "I felt happy when the Indians got blown up because they're bad guys," how can we know if she is suspending her political understandings of racism and colonialism in order to participate in the pleasure of watching this movie, or if the film has successfully interpellated her as the nonwhite, savage other who deserves to be defeated and colonized?

These problems of interpretation apply not just to impressionable, naive child viewers but to every situation in which people watch movies. Picture three women sitting in a theater watching a cinematic version of Jane Austen's *Emma*. One, who has already been interpellated hook, line, and sinker into patriarchy and middle-class aspirations, finds in the movie confirmation for her belief that the only way she can be happy and normal is to marry a man who is a good provider. Another viewer temporarily sets aside her critical stance on patriarchy and class privilege in real life and enjoys the film on its own terms, giving herself over to the logic of Austen's fictional world, in which a 20-year-old heroine's marriage to an aristocratic 38-year-old man is an emotionally satisfying outcome for the audience as well as for the characters. The third viewer, unwilling or unable to participate in the pleasures the film's narrative offers, sees it as a dangerous and offensive ideological tract that works to convince women that their happiness is to be found only in marriage to a rich and powerful man. Is the third viewer, who can't or won't separate her political beliefs from her enjoyment of the movie, more ideologically aware or sophisticated than the second? And how are we to tell the difference between viewer one, who doesn't know any better, and viewer two, who willingly suspends her disbelief in patriarchy and the inherent dignity of the landed classes in order to enjoy the film? The answer to these questions seems to be, "Just ask them." But as my analyses of interview transcripts have demonstrated so far, answers to such questions are not so easy for respondents to give or for researchers to interpret.

NORMATIVITY

Before getting back to the task of interpreting the children's responses to my questions about good guys and bad guys, I must introduce one more level of methodological complexity. This book is concerned with how children make sense of movies that are violent, sexist, racist, colonialist, and classbound. The chapters of the book follow this list of topics. But by looking at these issues one at a time, I risk missing the interconnections. In the focus group discussions of *Swiss Family Robinson*, as in real life, issues of class, race, colonialism, and gender are intertwined. Gay scholars have coined the term *heteronormativity* to refer (usually sarcastically and always critically) to straight, patriarchal notions of sex and gender. Alongside heteronormativity there are similarly rigid, normalizing notions of class, race, and culture. I use the word *normativity* here to refer to the confluence of these multiple normative domains. A lack of cross-disciplinary, cross-issue work is a failing of much of the scholarship on media representations of race, class, and gender. Too much of this scholarship focuses on just one of these issues in isolation from the others. Marxist media critics focus on class, feminists on gender, and African American and ethnic studies scholars on race and ethnicity. These competing theoretical and political interests and perspectives can be seen in the bitterness of the critical discussions that surrounded *The Cosby Show*. The program was praised by many critics who foreground race for providing positive role models for black children and breaking harmful racial stereotypes by presenting on network television a well-adjusted, economically and educationally successful African American family. On the other hand, critics who foreground class blasted the show for its valorization of middle-class values, while feminists pointed out that the show did little to break the mold of the patriarchal sitcom. Taken one issue or interest at a time, and without talking to actual viewers, it is easy to speak authoritatively about how the ideological messages embedded in a program like *The Cosby Show* will affect people. But in the real world, in local settings, and especially in the experience of children, race, class, and gender are not issues that come neatly packaged or that play out in predictable ways. (For a review of the *Cosby Show* debate, see Jhally & Lewis, 1992; for audience response studies of the program, see Sefton-Green, 1990, and Buckingham, 1993.)

How, then, to proceed? The thesis of this book is that ideological effects of the mass media are experienced by children according to their prior experiences and as mediated by their local ways of understanding and speaking about the world. *Swiss Family Robinson* presents a 1960s Hollywood version of violence, gender, class, and intercultural relations. The children at Koa make sense of this cinematic version of life by reading it alongside other texts, experiences, and discourses. If we are to understand how the children make sense of *Swiss Family Robinson*, what's needed, then, is an ethnography of their notions of normativity.

A TAXONOMY OF GOODNESS AND BADNESS

Up to this point, I've used textual modes of analysis borrowed from the humanities to analyze extended sections of interview transcripts. In this chapter, I employ as well a more traditional social science mode of analyzing qualitative data—content coding. To develop a sense of the range and organization of how the children at Koa conceptualize good and evil in *Swiss Family Robinson*, I decided to look at responses across the focus groups. I began this process by combining all the responses the children in the 32 groups offered to the question "How do you tell the difference between the good guys and the bad guys in *Swiss Family Robinson*?" This yielded a list of 182 comments. Working back and forth between the responses and my emerging classificatory scheme, collapsing and splitting categories until I could accommodate most of the responses, I came up with 11 binary categories—11 characteristics of good guys and a paired list of 11 characteristics of bad guys (see Table 5.1). The idea of organizing an ethnography around the identification of core binaries is informed by the work of structuralist anthropologists including Mary Douglas (1966) and Claude Lévi-Strauss (1969). Jacques Derrida (1992) urges us to look for the power relations in binary oppositions—inevitably, one pole of the binary will be dominant and privileged, the other pole subservient and degraded.

In turn, I locate these 11 binary categories within three supercategories or master narratives the children use to make sense of the differences between the good guys and bad guys in *Swiss Family Robinson*: (1) Manifest Destiny over recalcitrant savagery; (2) the middle-class family fending off the envious and unruly lower classes; and (3) domesticated versus predatory masculinity. These three master narratives overlap, but for the purposes of analysis, I'll take them one at a time. In this chapter, I explore how the children at Koa understand colonialism and what it means to be savage versus civilized. In Chapter 6, I look at the children's understandings of the inherent goodness of families, first with a focus on class issues, then on heteronormativity.

In addition to the focus group interviewing, I asked children in two

Table 5.1. Characteristics of good guys and bad guys.

Good Guys	Bad Guys
defend	attack (without provocation)
outnumbered	large numbers (a horde or a gang)
above	below
civilized and attractive	primitive and ugly
ingenious and resourceful	unplanful, hapless, pathetic
win	lose
domestic	nomadic
nice (face and clothes)	mean/junky (faces and clothes)
industrious and deserving	indolent and undeserving
animals and crops	no animals or crops
families	men without women and children

classes at Koa to draw pictures of a good guy and a bad guy from the film. I include examples of these drawings to illustrate the children's categorization of good and evil.

COLONIALISM'S CORE BINARIES

The crucial plot element that the Robinson Crusoe saga in each of its manifestations, including *Swiss Family Robinson*, shares with the Hollywood western is the ideological justification of colonialism. As Engelhardt (1987) suggests,

American movie-makers did not invent . . . the version of world history they present in their films. They must be given full credit, however, for developing a highly successful and satisfying cinematic form to encapsulate an existing ideological message. With this form they have been able to relegate the great horrors of Western expansion into the rest of the world, and of present-day American hegemony over great hunks of it, to another universe of pleasure and enjoyment. (p. 494)

In other words, the stakes are high when children watch films like *Swiss Family Robinson*. The popular and scholarly concern over imitative violence has a misplaced focus. Instead of counting violent acts in a movie, we should be attending to the way in which violence in films is located within a larger moral and ideological argument about justifiable uses of force against certain categories of people (Gerbner, 1970). For example, in the case of the *Mighty Morphin Power Rangers*, I am less concerned about children imitating the highly stylized karate movements of the Rangers than I am with how the TV program perpetuates the stereotype of the Asian dragon lady. In the original (Japanese) version of the show, both the Power Rangers and their adversaries are played by Japanese actors. But in the remade version shown in the West, the Rangers, when not wearing their masks, are played by Caucasian, Asian American and African American actors, while the chief villain, played by a Japanese actress (wearing makeup not unlike Sessue Hayakawa's in *Swiss Family Robinson*), has been dubbed into English rather than reshot with an American actress. By remaking the program in this way, a jingoistic, good-Americans-versus-evil-Orientals theme has been added (McLaren & Morris, 1997). I have a similar concern about violence in Teenage Mutant Ninja Turtles movies, where the likable and highly moral Turtles battle hordes of Japanese bad guys. My concern with violence in *Swiss Family Robinson* therefore has less to do with children mindlessly imitating the shooting, sword-wielding, and bomb-throwing in the movie than with the possibility that the movie's joyful presentation of the Robinsons' violence toward the Asian and Polynesian pirates might work to reinforce an ideological message that circulates in the larger society suggesting that wars of aggression against nonwhite, indigenous peoples are necessary and justified. George Gerbner (1970) has put forward the notion of *proposition analysis* as a way of describing how television programs propose a view of the world that justifies the mistreatment of certain categories of people.

Many of the children's responses to the interview question about how they tell the good guys from the bad guys seem to confirm Engelhardt's fears about the success of films like *Swiss Family Robinson* in selling a colonialist message to impressionable viewers. The students at Koa for the most part seem unable or unwilling to resist the film's colonialist take on the world. The key ideological conventions of both colonialism and the Hollywood Third World movie are captured neatly in a statement offered by 12-year-old Tisha: "The bad guys look bad, and they act really stupid, and they have a lot of people, and they usually kill people for no reason." Let's consider these components one at a time, looking for evidence of both interpellation and resistance.

Good Guys Defend, Bad Guys Attack

Colonizers have a knack for creating the illusion that they are the innocent, undeserving victims of unprovoked native violence. In both Hollywood movies and government press releases, colonizers' aggression against native peoples is invariably reconstrued as justified defensive action. In the *Swiss Family Robinson* saga, this mystification is supported by the plot device that puts the story into motion: as victims of a shipwreck, the Robinsons ostensibly are the unwilling, unintended stewards of an uninhabited tropical island. They had no intention to take anyone's land. It was an accident. But reading beneath this plot device, the Robinsons are clearly marked as complicit in the colonial project. Why was this Swiss family on a ship in the middle of the Indian Ocean with all their household possessions, tools, and farm animals if not to participate in the colonization of some native people's land? The movie tells us in passing that the Robinsons were shipwrecked while in transit to start a new life as settlers in New Guinea. This plot element is much more explicit in the novel on which the film is based. Johann David Wyss, like Daniel Defoe before him, avoids depicting the morally complex relations between European settlers and an agricultural native people by placing his protagonists on a uninhabited island and having them fight invading cannibals.

The Disney version of the story masks its underlying colonialist theme by making the Robinsons' adversaries not native peoples but pirates who, as nomads and thieves, have no justifiable claim to the island. The absence of any native inhabitants on this lush tropical island serves the colonial mystification that Europeans took over empty lands. Is there an island in the world with a perfect climate, abundant fruit and game, and unlimited fresh water that is unpopulated? By depicting the villains as Southeast Asian and Polynesian pirates, Disney's version of *Swiss Family Robinson* alludes to an indigenous population while avoiding the need to deal directly with colonialism. The battle scene works on two levels: pirates attacking an innocent, shipwrecked family, and colonizers repelling an attack by natives on the warpath.

What do the children at Koa make of all this? They seem to endorse the circular logic of the film (and of colonialism) that good guys only defend themselves and that people who defend themselves are good guys, as we can see in such focus group comments as "Good guys don't charge," "They only fight back, the good guys," "The good ones are on defense," "Good guys wouldn't just do something bad. They'd go on defense," "The good guys just wanted to make them go away, because they were saving themselves," and "The good guys always stay backed up, the bad guys always charge."

The use of sports metaphors ("the team on defense") is characteristic of how the children conceptualize both war and colonial encounters. Perhaps because team sports provide them with their first experience of intergroup conflict and within-group loyalty, children at Koa tend to understand battles between colonizers and natives in terms of team sports competitions (see Figure 5.1). Organized team sports—baseball and soccer for boys, soccer for girls—are very big in the Koa community. The linking of sports and war is a metaphor that is common in American society, where football coaches use

Figure 5.1. Good guys and bad guys as opposing sports teams.

the language of military tactics to describe their game plans ("The game is going to be won or lost in the trenches") and generals use sports metaphors to explain military tactics ("We used our tanks to run an end-around on Saddam").

The metaphoric linking of colonial encounters and sports is especially appropriate at Koa, which sits within eyesight of Aloha Stadium. On Saturday evenings in the fall, the university football team, the Rainbow Warriors, is led onto the field by a cheerleader dressed as a hypermuscular, nearly naked, traditional Hawaiian warrior, wearing a gourd helmet on his head and brandishing a koa spear. The older children are well aware of the excitement that is felt throughout Hawai'i on weekends when the team, featuring a roster of local Hawaiian and Polynesian players, takes on an opponent from the mainland. It is as if these sports encounters give local people in Hawai'i a chance to redress colonial, plantation-era, and territorial wrongs.

In the focus group discussions, the Koa children used their understanding of team sports to make the interracial fighting in *Swiss Family Robinson* both more understandable and less horrifying. For instance, several children obliquely referred to the racial difference between the all-White Robinsons and the Asian and Polynesian pirates by using the concept of competing teams wearing contrasting uniforms:

INTERVIEWER: How did they make the bad guys and the good guys look different?

ASHLEY: They made them different colors and made them have different kinds of weapons.

INTERVIEWER: How did they make them different colors?

DESIREE: Oh, I know why they made them look like bad guys and good guys, because they were charging each other, one team was on one side, and the other team . . .

ASHLEY: One side could have been good guys and one of them could have been bad guys.

INTERVIEWER: Do you think pirates really look like that?

ASHLEY: Sometimes.

AMANDA: I don't think so. I think the bad guys should all wear one of those red belts like Jennifer's, like a red string, and a white shirt and black pants.

Amanda seems to be suggesting that the movie could be improved by having the pirate "team" dress more uniformly. She would find it easier to keep the sides straight if all the pirates would dress, like her friend Jennifer or the Pirates of Penzance, in black pants, white shirts, and red belts.

Children at Koa also bring the tensions of the movie into their realm of understanding and thereby take some of the sting out of the colonial encounter by understanding the Robinsons' battle with the pirates in terms of a schoolyard disagreement. Many of the children reported that in the movie, as on the playground, the bad guys are "the ones who started it," and the good guys are "the ones who were just defending themselves." Stephanie takes this primary school logic one step further. Speaking in the register of the Solomonlike teacher, she chastizes the Robinsons as well as the pirates: "I think they were both bad, because they were both throwing at each other and stuff and they didn't try to stop it or anything." In other words, even if the pirates started it, the Robinsons are equally to blame for responding to violence. In this familiar classroom management discourse, which many of the children seem to have internalized, right and wrong have to do not with the substantive reasons children fight, countries go to war, or colonized people rebel, but with who hit first and who retaliated in an encounter.

The children's use of the logic of team sports (offense and defense) and playground squabbles (who started it) to understand the violence in *Swiss Family Robinson* is tricky to assess. On one hand, these metaphors, by attributing similar motivations and interests to the nonwhite, shirtless pirates and the nicely dressed White family, can be seen as a way of questioning the film's manifest argument that the pirates are bloodthirsty savages and the Robinsons their peace-loving victims. Seeing both the pirates and the Robinsons as squabbling children or opposing football teams is a way of putting the savage and civilized characters in the film on a more equal footing and thereby undercutting the film's racism. On the other hand, these metaphors encourage a sanitized take on the colonial dynamics that are implied by the film at a deeper level of meaning. A problem with applying the sports metaphor to the battle scene in *Swiss Family Robinson* is that it elides the inequality and the nonvoluntary nature of colonial encounters—colonialism isn't a fair fight between well-matched teams testing their abilities on a level playing field. The frequency with which the children at Koa used sports analogies to make sense of the violence in *Swiss Family Robinson* suggests to me that perhaps as educators we should be doing more to help students understand how sporting events are unlike wars and how wars are unlike sporting events.

Good Guys Are Outnumbered

Perhaps one reason the good guys never attack is that they are always outnumbered. Children in many of the groups explained that they can tell who is good and who is bad by who has the numerical advantage: "Usually I can just tell the bad guys 'cause they, the bad guys, usually have more men and the good guys have less," "'Cause the ones who attacked the Americans, they had only a little bit and they had plenty," and "The good guys were so little and the bad guys were so much people" (see Figure 5.2). Here again, the children's responses reveal a tendency to understand the violence in *Swiss Family Robinson* using the logic of the schoolyard dispute: bad guys, like bad children, don't fight fair—they gang up on their victims.

The film presents the Robinsons as being overrun by a horde of savages. Linking moral superiority with being fewer in numbers is a favorite mystification of both colonial regimes and the movies Hollywood makes to honor them. In *Unthinking Eurocentrism* (1994), Ella Shohat and Robert Stam describe this logic as "the colonial proportion," which

> decrees that many of "them" must die for each one of "us," a pattern repeated in films of Zulus fighting the British, Mexicans fighting the U.S. cavalry, American soldiers against Japanese kamikaze bombers, and, most recently, American pilots against Iraqi conscripts. (p. 120)

We find the colonial proportion in accounts of the handful of Texans and other White Americans defending their fort against thousands of Mexicans at

Figure 5.2. The 4 good guys, on the right side of the picture, have bodies and faces. They are outnumbered by the bad guys on the left of the picture who are drawn as nearly identical stick figures.

the Alamo; Custer and his small band of men ambushed by thousands of Sioux at Little Big Horn; the 600 horsemen of the Light Brigade being mowed down by thousands of Turks; a garrison of the French Foreign Legion defending a desert outpost against a Moslem horde; and a few British soldiers and Boers fighting side by side against thousands of spear-chucking tribesmen in the Zulu wars. What these stories of brave, hopelessly outnumbered colonial martyrs elide is that the whole point of colonialism is for a few people from the First World to dominate thousands from the Third. The colonizers are always outnumbered, not because the natives are ganging up on them, but because that is how colonialism is meant to operate. When the natives sporadically fight back by attacking the barracks, the fort, or the supply depot of an occupying army, the ideology of colonialism encourages the martyrdom of the slain soldiers and uses the villainy of the colonized people's sneak attack to justify harsh countermeasures, including an increase in the size of the colonizing army and the ruthlessness of their rule.

In Hollywood movies, the countermeasures classically take the form of the beleaguered garrison or circled wagon train being saved by the cavalry. Because colonialism succeeds in establishing the lie that the colonizers are the overwhelmed, outnumbered victims of native aggression, the slaughter of thousands of underarmed native people by a decidedly militarily superior force of cavalry (or the Royal Navy, or paratroopers, or Green Berets, or jets with sidewinder missiles and napalm) becomes, in film if not always in real life, a morally righteous and thus pleasurable event to behold.

The Robinsons are saved, not by the cavalry, but by the arrival of a British naval gunship that blasts the fleeing pirates out of the water. The fourth-graders we met in Chapter 3 made an intertextual association between *Swiss Family Robinson* and the Hollywood western as they brought Indians and the cavalry into their discussion:

INTERVIEWER: What gave you a clue about who were the bad guys and who were the good guys?

CLEM: Because usually the bad guys come, they keep on charging, and the good guys don't, the good guys don't charge.

BRANSON: They wear the knife thing, and the costume.

SHIRLEY: Usually the bad guys dress darker than the good guys, and the good guys dress lighter.

JEWEL: And they were a family. The bad guys weren't.

FRANK: They were just a big group. And I could tell they were the bad guys because there was more and the other guys were a little bit. There was only about five people on the good guys' team and like a hundred on the bad guys'.

CLEM: Two thousand!

INTERVIEWER: In the other movies that you watch, is it easy to tell who are the good guys?
SHIRLEY: Yeah.
BRANSON: Especially in the cavalry.
FRANK: Especially in cartoons. I like, in the X-Men you can tell that, there's cards on the back that says if they're bad.
BRANSON: I'm rooting for the cavalry.
CLEM: Hey, Branson. I don't care for the cavalry. It isn't good because the White people . . . I like the Indians.
JEWEL: The Indians were just trying to defend themselves, the White people were the ones who brought all the bad traits and all that.
SHIRLEY: I don't know. Indians are not called Indians.
INTERVIEWER: Did you feel sorry for anyone?
EVERYONE: No.
INTERVIEWER: Not even when the logs were falling on them?
FRANK: They shouldn't be attacking in the first place.

This conversation presents a rich combination of most of the content categories children at Koa use to distinguish good guys from bad guys. We have the metaphor of team sports ("the good guys' team," dark and light uniforms) and the suggestion that the bad guys are the ones who attack without warning or provocation while the good guys are the family who are outnumbered. But the introduction to the discussion of the cavalry opens up an opportunity for an anticolonialist counterargument to emerge. In the course of providing examples of characters in movies and on TV who can immediately be identified as the good guys, Branson suggests "the cavalry." Presumably, he is referring here to the last-minute heroic arrival of the cavalry in a Hollywood western. But by supplementing his comment with the phrase, "I'm rooting for the cavalry," Branson creates a discursive space for Clem to counter, "I like the Indians." "Rooting" is another example of the children drawing on their knowledge of sports events to understand violence in movies. But just as people at sports events root for both sides, so in this conversation Clem, who is one of a handful of African American children at Koa, announces that he is a supporter of the home team—the Indians—rather than the visitors—the (White) cavalry.

Jewel follows Clem's statement about preferring the Indians to the calvalry by saying that "the White people were the ones who brought all the bad traits and all that." I read this comment as a reference both to the bad moral character of colonizers and to the diseases brought by soldiers, sailors, and settlers to Native Americans on the U.S. mainland and to Native Hawaiians in Hawai'i. The fourth-grade Hawaiian studies curriculum includes discussion of the precipitous decline of the Hawaiian population in the immediate postcontact period caused by the introduction of western diseases. My hunch is that schoolchildren, who are very susceptible to contagious diseases, find this notion of colonizers bringing diseases to vulnerable native peoples a powerful counterargument to the usual curricular and media representations of colonialism as heroic discovery and the progress of civilization. The anticolonialist statements by Clem and Jewel strike a chord in Shirley, reminding her of the politically correct message she heard, perhaps in a social studies lesson in school, that "Indians are not called Indians." Her "I don't know" suggests that she doesn't know where she stands on the issues Clem and Jewel have introduced, but she does know that the whole topic of colonial history and native people's rights has to be discussed gingerly.

How significant is this flurry of anticolonial sentiment? When the interviewer proceeds to ask them about their emotional response to the film ("Did you feel sorry for anyone?") the group collectively replies "No," and Frank justifies this answer with the familiar colonial argument that these natives/pirates shouldn't have been on the warpath in the first place. This may suggest that while watching the film, all the children, including Clem and Jewel, found pleasure in the Robinsons' success in repelling their attackers. I suspect that when they say "No, we didn't feel sorry for the pirates," Clem and Jewel are being honest about their emotional response to the film. But finding pleasure in the film's action doesn't necessarily mean that they have been interpellated by the film's ideological take on the world. The discussion suggests that once the film stops running, Clem and Jewel are able to marshal counterdiscourses that effectively question the film's colonial message.

The Bad Guys Are Below, the Good Guys Above

Colonialism imagines the peoples of the world as links in the Great Chain of Being. At the top of this chain is God. Just below God comes Angels, then White Europeans. Next come South Asians, Arabs, Chinese, and other peoples who once had great cultures before falling into decay. Then come Native Americans and Polynesians, then Blacks, then the great apes, and so on down through the animal kingdom. The notion of the Great Chain of Being links the colonial enterprise to the racist branch of evolutionary theory. When the bad guys attack the good guys from below, they are attempting to climb up the rungs of the evolutionary ladder. This is the core visual image of colonialism—the civilized good guys above, the savage bad guys below. In *The Empire's Old Clothes* (1983), Ariel Dorfman exposes the centrality of the trope of rising in the Babar books. Babar, once saved from primitivism by the Old Lady, is continuously rising as he flies in balloons, soars as the elephants' Santa, dwells in his house on the hill, and even literally rides on the backs of his subjects.

Children in the focus groups offered several statements suggesting that they know how to read the spatial locations of the pirates and the Robinsons in the film as a coded language signifying civilization versus savagery and good versus evil: "The good guys are the ones above," "The bad guys are below," "The bad guys are the ones coming up," and "The good guys was the family on top of the mountain. And the pirates, they're trying to come up and get them" (see Figure 5.3). Are these just straightforward, insightful readings of the visual grammar of the film, or does the ease with which children employ "up" and "down" as descriptors for the pirates and the Robinsons suggest that the film is successfully tapping into and perhaps even strengthening preexisting notions the children hold about racial hierarchies?

Civilized and Attractive Versus Primitive and Ugly

Support for the racial hierarchy argument can be found in comments the children made about the primitiveness of the pirates, who are described as stupid, lacking the ability to use complicated tools (as the Robinsons do), and swarthy, hairy, and generically ethnic: "The bad guys are the ones with hair on their face," "The bad guys are the darker ones," "The bad guys have no teeth, no front teeth," "They look ugly, like they have scars, and bald heads, and mustaches." In other words, the less a character in a film looks like a clean-shaven, nicely dressed northern European who has had good dental work, the more dangerous and primitive he appears to the children.

I suspect that in addition to their "war party" mode of attack, it is their bare-chestedness that most contributes to the pirates' being mistaken for Indians. Being properly covered up has long been a hallmark that colonizing nations use to distinguish themselves from natives and savages. White people introduced not just Christianity and capitalism but also the ankles-to-neck mu'umu'u to Hawai'i. Dorfman (1983) provides a telling example of the significance of putting on clothes in his analysis of the Babar stories. Dorfman points out that young children readily identify with the primitiveness of the naked elephants who walk on all fours because children themselves only recently got up on two legs and acquired a sense of embarrassment about nudity. Thus the phylogeny of the rise of civilization is repeated in the ontogeny of child development. *Swiss Family Robinson* uses this binary of the dressed and the undressed to signify not just the opposition between good and evil but also between civilization and barbarism. The children at Koa show that they know how to read these dress codes when they say that the good guys were "[the ones] in white shirts," and "a girl wearing a black dress and the boys wearing long pants and a t-shirt." In other transcripts the children spoke similarly: "You can tell the pirates, they were all bald like that, and they didn't have any shirts, and they looked ugly and they had missing teeth, and

Figure 5.3. On the left side of the drawing, the good guys send the bad guys flying back down the mountain. On the right side, the father and son drop coconut bombs onto the pirates below.

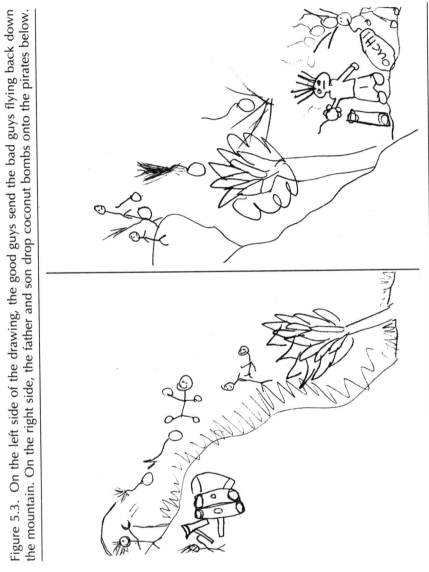

they had swords"; "[You could tell by] the way they looked—they had no shirts and they were mostly bald."

We must keep in mind that these comments linking race, ethnicity, clothing, and physical appearance to evil were offered in the context of talking about the semiotics of *Swiss Family Robinson*. While it is disturbing that the children at Koa seem comfortable talking about goodness and evil in terms of physical appearance, clothing, and body types, over the years I've spent in the classrooms and on the playground at Koa, I've seen little to suggest that this is how the Koa children judge themselves or each other.

Sophisticated and Effective Versus Hapless and Pathetic

There is some evidence in the interview transcripts to suggest that the children are not entirely comfortable with the film's equation of goodness with being White, above, and more civilized. One example is the response of a coed group of fifth-graders to our question, Who were the good guys?:

DANE: The people cutting the logs, and . . .
JENNIFER: The people who were on top of the hill.
RAELYN: The people who were trying to kill.

Continuing the singsong cadence developed by her classmates in the first two lines, Raelyn repeats Dane and Jennifer's sentence structure and then rounds things off by rhyming "hill" with "kill." Raelyn's inclusion of the word *kill* works to complicate the film's narrative of one-dimensional good and evil. Just as it is accurate to describe the Robinsons as cutting logs and being on top of the hill, so it is accurate to describe them as "trying to kill." If the Robinsons were on trial for manslaughter, the elaborately constructed traps they built would certainly suggest premeditated (though perhaps justifiable) intent to maim or kill. By stating aloud this simple truth—that the Robinsons are a killing machine—Raelyn effectively destabilizes the colonialist fiction of the film that the outnumbered good guys are the victims.

For the children at Koa, the coconut bomb was clearly the single most compelling element of the movie. When we asked, "What did you like best about the movie?" children invariably replied, "The coconut bomb!" In their drawings of the good guys in the film, a majority of the children included the coconut bomb (see Figure 5.4). Several of their pictures were of coconut bombs with no people present, the bomb functioning metonymically to represent the family (see Figure 5.5). Part of the excitement surrounding the coconut bombs, I think, has to do with the fact that it was the Robinsons' youngest child, rather than the older boys or the father, who concocted and threw them. It makes sense that child viewers would most enthusiastically identify with

Figure 5.4. A good guy throwing coconut bombs.

the exploits of the only child character in the movie. I suspect that the familiarity of coconuts to the children at Koa made this particular prop even more exciting to them than it might be to audiences in coconut-free settings.

A bomb (even if it's made from a coconut) is a complex symbol to use in a children's movie. Of the various weapons the Robinsons used against the pirates, the coconut bomb produced not just the most enthusiastic response but also the most varied and resistant readings in the Koa children. The prob-

Figure 5.5. The coconut bomb represents the good guys metonymically. This artist may have confused a coconut with a pineapple. But I'm inclined to give the artist credit for using the cross-hatching to suggest a hybrid between a coconut and a hand-grenade.

Good guy

lem is that "bombing" just doesn't go well with "good guys." My hunch is that bombs are so terrifying to children and so difficult to associate with honor, virtue, and defensive military actions that the coconut bomb in *Swiss Family Robinson* functions as a point of slippage in the children's reading of the movie. The Robinsons' coconut bomb is a complex signifier: it is part sophisticated strategic weapon dropped from above, like the "smart" bombs used against Iraq and Serbia, and it is part homemade explosive, like the bombs concocted by the IRA, the World Trade Center bombers, Timothy McVeigh, and Theodore Kaczynski. It is the Robinsons' coconut bombing of the pirates that produced the most excitement in the children, but also the most uncertainty about who were the victims and who were the aggressors in the movie.

For example, when asked "Who were the bad guys?" Ryan, a first-grader, responded: "The pirates, and they're trying to come up, and they have exploding bombs." It is unclear whether Ryan's second "they" is meant to refer to the Robinsons or to the pirates. Either way, his statement suggests some tension and confusion about whether the guys using "exploding bombs" are good or bad. A similar sense of tension and confusion is apparent in this exchange among three second-graders:

INTERVIEWER: Who were good guys?
MOANA: The ones on the hill, who was dropping down the logs and the co-
conut bombs and stuff.
LISA: But one team didn't have any bombs or anything.
MONIQUE: The bad guys were dead and the good guys were killing them.

Moana's comment suggests that the logs the Robinsons dropped on the pirates were sufficiently bomblike to raise some of the same questions in the children's minds as did the coconut bombs. Monique's parallel construction in the two clauses of her sentence works effectively to emphasize a key point that the movie attempts to soft-pedal: it is the bad guys who got killed and the good guys who did the killing. Lisa, conceptualizing the battle in sports terms, is bothered by the inequity of one team's being less well equipped than the other. The ragtag, originally hapless, multiethnic sports team that gets beaten badly by an all-White, middle-class, much better equipped team is a very popular genre of children's film. Although the Robinsons are outnumbered, they are better armed, better dressed, better coached, blonder, and better looking than the pirates. My hunch is that when the Robinsons are too effective in defeating the pirates, and particularly when they use the bombs and logs, their status as good guys is compromised by their intertextual similarity to the bad guys in films such as *The Bad News Bears* and *The Mighty Ducks*. This is an inherent artistic problem of films that attempt to sell colonialism—in presenting the good guys as more intelligent, better organized, and more technologically sophisticated and the bad guys as stupid, childlike, and primitive, colonialist films such as *Swiss Family Robinson* risk creating sympathy for the bungling natives and antipathy for the efficient colonizers.

The coconut bomb frequently was the subject of arguments within groups about who was good and who was bad:

INTERVIEWER: Who were the bad guys?
KASIA: The people who were throwing the bomb. So they could die.
MITCHELL: No. I think the good guys were the ones throwing the bombs,
    'cause the bad guys they, good people, they don't get Indians and all
    these people to kill them.
INTERVIEWER: Were those Indians?
MITCHELL: Yeah. They had funny hair, they dressed funny, and they had
    mean faces.
AMBER: If the bad guys were the ones throwing bombs, they wouldn't have
    little kids with them.

Here Mitchell and Amber use tautological arguments to counter Kasia's suggestion that the Robinsons were the bad guys because they were killing people
with bombs. Mitchell's reasoning gets a bit garbled, but the point he makes
is an interesting one: the Robinsons must be the good people in the movie
because bad guys don't get attacked by bad guys (Indians). I think the problem Mitchell has with the syntax of his sentence is a symptom of the complicated logic he is employing here. His reasoning is circular and thus not entirely convincing. And yet, from the point of view of cinematic genre analysis,
it is reasonable to suggest that one way directors mark good guys as good
guys is to have them be attacked by bad guys. Amber, echoing Mitchell's
approach, seems to be suggesting that although they threw the bombs, the
Robinsons must be the good guys because they are the ones with children on
their side, and in films of this genre, children are markers of goodness.

Because we showed them only a three-minute segment from near the end
of the movie, children who hadn't seen *Swiss Family Robinson* before had no
way of knowing why the pirates were attacking the Robinsons. This was an
intended feature of my method—I wanted to learn how children read aspects
of movies other than the plot to identify good and bad characters. Earlier
events in the movie suggest that the pirates' primary motivation was to recap-
ture and presumably rape a British Navy captain's daughter whom the older
Robinson boys had liberated and brought back to the treehouse. Even those
children at Koa who had seen the whole film were confused by this aspect of
the plot, as they were not entirely clear about why the captain, anticipating
the arrival of the pirates, had cut his daughter's hair and dressed her to look
like a boy. Raelyn and Loreen took a stab at explaining this plot element to
the other children in their group the second time I interviewed them:

CASSIDY: Can we watch the whole movie this time?
RAELYN: I like this movie. It's a Disney thing. *Walt Disney Presents.* He's
    trying to kill the little girl.
LOREEN: They're trying to kill the little girl, but they think it's a boy.

RAELYN: Yeah, before this she got dressed as a boy because the pirates like
to kill girls and they don't like to kill boys.

Raelyn's comment gives us some insight into how children read adult plot
elements in movies. Raelyn and Loreen are old enough to understand that the
teenage girl's gender makes her an object of the pirate's desire, but they are
young enough to conceptualize this desire as an intent to kill her rather than
to use her sexually. The notion that the lower orders of human beings are
after the women of the White higher classes is a key theme of colonialist
discourse. The filmmakers responsible for *Swiss Family Robinson* slipped this
generic plot element of the colonialist film into the script, but it seems to
have gone over the heads of most of the children at Koa. The desire of dark,
primitive men for White girls and women is present in the film to adult viewers, but, from my reading of the transcripts, absent, at least on a conscious
level, to child viewers.

Lacking an understanding of the pirates' motivation for attacking the
Robinsons, some of the children were unconvinced that the pirates deserved
the harsh treatment doled out to them by the bomb-throwing Robinsons:

INTERVIEWER: Who were the good guys?
SADE: The people who threw the coconuts.
MELISSA: Not the people who were throwing the bombs, the people who
were walking up the hill.
INTERVIEWER: What makes you think that?
MELISSA: Because they weren't throwing bombs or anything.
INTERVIEWER: What were they doing?
MELISSA: Just walking. Probably they just got into a fight.
SADE: Maybe they must have stole something from them.
INTERVIEWER: Who did you feel sorry for?
ASHLEY: The good guys.
MELISSA: The bad guys.
INTERVIEWER: Why?
SOPHIA: Because they're dead.
MELISSA: We should be sorry for them because they didn't really do any-
thing and they died.

Melissa was by no means alone in feeling sorry for the pirates. "Did you feel
sorry for anyone in the movie?" proved to be the most controversial question
we asked in that it produced the most divided answers. Typically, as in the
conversation reported above, at least one child (most often a girl) would express sympathy for one or more of the pirates (most often for the "bolo-head"
or bald pirate, who repeatedly got hit in the head by logs) and then another

child would counter, "I felt happy when he got hit because he was a bad guy." The film works hard to prevent such sympathetic reactions by using such devices as cutting away before the Robinsons' projectiles reach their target, not showing any blood or other signs that the Robinsons' weapons have any lasting effect, and scoring the battle scene with light-hearted music and comical sound effects. Nevertheless, many of the Koa children were disturbed by the violence inflicted by the Robinsons on the pirates.

I would suggest that disagreements within groups about whether one should feel sorry for the pirates are more usefully understood as a reflection of contradictions in the film and the inherently ambivalent experience of watching action movies than as a sign of individual psychological differences among the children. My hunch is that the children who said they didn't feel sorry for the pirates while watching the movie were providing an honest retroactive description of the way they felt as movie watchers who had given themselves over to the pleasures of the movie. In response to the question, "Did you feel sorry for anyone?" Teresa, a third-grader, was refreshingly direct about admitting the pleasure to be found in watching the bad guys in movies get their just desserts: "It gave me a good feeling."

When I asked the "Chinese eyes" group how they felt when the logs were hitting the pirates, Loreen responded "Funny." Several children used "funny" in this way, perhaps to indicate both that they found the experience of watching the fight scene pleasurable (fun) and that they identified the genre of the movie as comedy, which would explain why they didn't feel sorry for anyone. Other children expressed the other side of the experience of watching a film in which things happen that we find disturbing in real life: "I felt sorry for the bolo-head man cuz that would hurt if it was real." Action films, like horror films, require a willing suspension of disbelief and, sometimes, of political and social concerns as well. To the degree that they could set aside their concern for people being hurt in real life, the children at Koa could enjoy the scene I showed them. The pleasures of the scene were less available to children for whom the violence felt real and to those who were offended by the film's depiction of a family of White settlers mowing down an army of people of color.

The Good Guys Are the Ones Who Win

Responses to our question, "How do you know who were the good guys?" included: "That's easy. Because the good guys always win," "Always the good guys win," "The ones that was winning," and "We just know—whoever is winning." This is another example of the tautological reasoning children employ to distinguish the good guys from the bad guys. But this tautology, rather than indicating sloppy or immature thinking on the children's part,

shows that they are in tune with the "victor's justice" logic of colonialism as
well as with the generic conventions of the children's action film. In real life,
one can't always figure out who are the good guys and the bad guys by
waiting to see who wins. But this logic works well when applied to identifying the good guys in certain film genres, as Stevie, a third-grader, explained:

INTERVIEWER: How could you tell they were the bad guys?
STEVIE: Because they were losing.
INTERVIEWER: That's not always true, is it?
STEVIE: It is, like, in cartoons.

"Good people always win in the end and the people who win in the end
are good" is the moral logic not just of cartoons and Disney movies, but also
of colonialism. The Puritan settlers in North America argued that their
worldly success was proof of God's approval. And the success of the young
American nation in taking over big chunks of the North American continent
from Native Americans and from the Spanish, French, and British was evidence of the justness and rightness of colonialist expansion—the farther west
and south the United States successfully ventured, the more logical, inevitable, and right became the dream of Manifest Destiny. The same logic applies
to the Robinsons, whose ingenuity, technological know-how, bravery, and
success testify to their moral superiority. The Robinsons win because they are
the good guys, and they are good guys because they win. Just as God
wouldn't let the Puritans or Americans prosper if they weren't good, so Walt
Disney Productions wouldn't let the Robinsons win if they were not the
proper and deserving heroes of the movie.

Most of the children we interviewed bought into this logic. Most, but not
all. When we showed the tape to the Hawaiian-language immersion students
at Koa, except for the fact that the interviews were conducted in Hawaiian,
the responses were much the same as in the English-language classrooms.
Most of the Hawaiian-language students readily identified the Robinson family as the good guys and the pirates as the bad guys. Only 9-year-old Punihei
Kameʻeleihiwa, the daughter of Lilikalā Kameʻeleihiwa, who is a professor
of Hawaiian studies and a leader in the sovereignty movement, expressly dis-
agreed:

LILINOE (Interviewer): ʻO wai nā
poʻe maikaʻi?
MAKANA: A, nā kānaka haole.
PUNIHEI: Noʻonoʻo wau, aʻole maopopo inā no ke aha aia kēlā mau kānaka ma ko lākou ʻāina, akā aia

LILINOE: Who are the good guys?

MAKANA: The *haole* guys.
PUNIHEI: I think, I don't know if,
why were those people on their
land, but maybe that was their land.

paha kēlā ko lākou ʻāina a ua hoʻāʻo
nā haole e hele mai a lawe a ʻo ia
ke kumu ua hele mai lākou a e mā-
lama kālewa.

LILINOE: Pehea kēlā manaʻo?

MOANI: Kumu, manaʻo wau ua
stranded lākou i ka ʻāina a laila hele
mai lākou no ka mea loaʻa kekahi
treasure ma ʻō e lawe a laila, akā,
ke hoʻāʻo nei lākou e kiʻi ia akā manaʻo nā poʻe ʻino, kēlā kāne, kēlā
mau kānaka he nui, manaʻo lākou ke
hoʻāʻo nei lākou e lawe i ko lākou
kula. Akā ʻaʻole lākou maopopo he
kula i ʻō.

LILINOE: Pehea ʻoukou e maopopo
ai ʻo wai nā poʻe maikaʻi, ʻo wai nā
poʻe ʻino?

IKAIKA: Nā poʻe maikaʻi e *defend*
iā lākou iho ma ka liko ana i ka
make.

LILINOE: Pehea ko ʻoukou nāʻau ke
heleleʻi, ʻolokaʻa nā kumu niu ma
luna o nā poʻe a i ʻole ka hoʻopohā
ʻana o nā pohā niu?

MAKANA: Maikaʻi. ʻAkaʻaka.

PUNIHEI: ʻAʻole maopopo iaʻu, no
ka mea, ʻaʻole maopopo he aha ka
mea maoli akā ʻano ʻino ke k̄iloi
ʻana inā ia ko lākou ʻāina.

And the *haoles* tried to come and
take it and that's why they came to
save it.

LILINOE: What do you think?

MOANI: Teacher, I think they were
stranded on the land and then *they*
came because there was some treasure there to take. And then, but,
when they tried to get it, but the bad
guys, that man, all those men, they
thought they were trying to take
their gold. But they didn't know
there was gold there.

LILINOE: How do you know who
are the good guys and who were the
bad guys?

IKAIKA: The good guys tried to defend themselves from death.

LILINOE: How did you feel when
the coconut trunks rolled down on
the people or when the coconut
bombs exploded?

MAKANA: Good. Funny.

PUNIHEI: I don't know because I
don't know what's real, but that
throwing is kind of mean if it's their
land.

Punihei's comment about *haoles* coming to take other people's land
("that was their land. And the *haoles* tried to come and take it") can be read
not just as an effective questioning and destabilizing of the movie's colonialist
ideology, but also as a paraphrase of the title and argument of her mother's
book, *Native Land and Foreign Desires* (1992), an account of the dispossession of Hawaiians from their land in the 19th century. I read Punihei's comment "that throwing [coconut bombs] is kind of mean if it's their land" as
referring obliquely to a more recent struggle: the effort of Hawaiian activists
to force the U.S. Navy to stop using the island of Kahoʻolawe as a target
range for heavy ordinance.

Of the 40 Hawaiian-language immersion students we interviewed, only one explicitly resisted the racist and colonialist ideology of *Swiss Family Robinson*. This statistic could be taken as evidence that this movie and others like it have been successful in interpellating these Hawaiian children into seeing themselves and their people as savages who have no just claim to their land. Although I am concerned about this possibility, I have a less pessimistic take. My hunch is that the Hawaiian children who identified the *haoles* as the good guys were speaking not about how they view goodness in real life, but rather about how goodness is defined within the world of the movie. Just as Lacey explained to me that Disney represents evil by giving actors exaggerated Asian features, I believe that these Hawaiian-language immersion students were explaining that within the plot of this movie the White people are good and the dark-skinned pirates are bad. That's how this movie works. It would be difficult to understand and enjoy this film in any other way. I know from other discussions with Hawaiian-language immersion students and their teachers that many of these children have sophisticated understandings of land and race in Hawai'i. Many are children of parents who are active in the sovereignty movement. Many have participated in marches and protests over the seizure of Hawaiian lands and the future of Hawaiian-language immersion education. Yet my research suggests that for better or worse, when these children watch movies like *Swiss Family Robinson*, they tend to put aside their political concerns about land and race in Hawai'i and cheer for the good White people and boo and laugh at the evil, bungling people of color.

It is a cause of concern that Punihei was the only child in the Hawaiian-language immersion program who seems to have been unable or unwilling to set aside her political understandings of the real world while watching and discussing *Swiss Family Robinson*. (Others may have had similar thoughts that they didn't express.) But the fact that one child we interviewed from the Hawaiian-language immersion program articulated a resistant position on the racism of the film can be viewed more optimistically. I think it is useful to think of Punihei as articulating a position on race and land in Hawai'i that is part of the local discourse at Koa. Punihei's was a lone voice in this particular discussion, but the concerns she raised are known to most of the children at Koa and are familiar to all but the youngest children in the Hawaiian-language immersion program. Solitary voices can have significant effects when the words spoken express the experiences and concerns of a significant group within the community of listeners. Colonialist and racist ideological messages are less likely to have harmful effects in local contexts where effective counterdiscourses circulate and where children have day-to-day experiences of interracial and interethnic interaction that contradict the one-dimensional interactions portrayed in the popular media.

The preponderance of the Koa children's statements about good guys and bad guys in *Swiss Family Robinson* gives us cause for concern that children are vulnerable to reactionary ideological messages in well-made films featuring attractive White heroes and repulsive dark villains. The children at Koa clearly know how to read the semiotics, iconography, and generic conventions of the colonialist action film: they know that the people in these films who are Whiter, better dressed, more closely shaven, higher up, and more technologically sophisticated are the good guys. They understand that the pleasure films of this genre have to offer is to be found in enjoying the victory of the heroic, defending colonizers over the attacking savage horde. And for the most part, although by no means unanimously, they report being able to put aside any sympathy they may be inclined to feel for the pirates and relish the Robinsons' victory.

But their capitulation to the logic and emotions of this colonialist saga is incomplete. In many of the focus group discussions, there was evidence of slippage between the ideological messages the film sends out and the meanings the local kids at Koa receive. This slippage was manifested in slips ("The bad guys were the ones with the bombs, I mean the good guys had the bombs"), in expressions of ambivalence ("I know the pirates were bad, but I still felt kind of sorry for them"), and in intragroup disagreements ("No, not the people who were throwing the bombs, the people who were walking up the hill"). The children tend to understand the warfare and colonial dynamics of the film in terms of their experience with team sports and schoolyard disputes. The use of these metaphors leads some of the children to criticize the pirates (who have numbers on their side) and some the Robinsons (who have the bomb) for enjoying an unfair advantage over the other (as if fair play applies to war and colonialism). Explicit resistance to the colonialist ideology of the film was rare but by no means nonexistent. Statements by an African American child who told his group that he cheers for the Indians against the cavalry and of a Native Hawaiian child who questioned how the Robinsons came to own their land were significant in presenting counterdiscourses to the core colonialist assumptions of the film.

CHAPTER 6

The Embattled Middle-Class Family

A group of 7- and 8-year-old girls discusses *Swiss Family Robinson*:

INTERVIEWER: Who were the good guys?
TASHA: The son and the daddy and the mommy and the big brother.
LIA: The ones who lived in the treehouse.
SHANNON: The ones with the nice faces.
INTERVIEWER: Who were the bad guys?
LIA: The men that tried to attack them.
SHANNON: The men that got killed.
INTERVIEWER: How did you know they were the bad guys?
SHANNON: They were ugly.
TASHA: They had clothes that were like junk.
CHERYL: They had all their weapons.
LIA: And the good guys were all staying in their place.

As its title suggests, *Swiss Family Robinson* is quintessentially a family movie. The hero of the film is not an individual, but the family as a unit. Much of the action of the film is domestic, as we watch the Robinsons build, decorate, and maintain their treehouse homestead. Unlike middle-class fathers in real life, but in keeping with the representation of such idealized fathers as those played by Robert Young in *Father Knows Best* and Bill Cosby on *The Cosby Show,* John Mills's "Father" Robinson is almost always around to give advice, solve problems, and respond to emergencies. Tensions in the plot, other than the Robinsons' battle with the pirates, are like those in a family sitcom—the little boy's earnest but comical efforts to be taken seriously by his parents and older siblings; the older boys' competition over the girl they both like; the antics of the family's collection of exotic pets; the mother's desire that the treehouse be homey and nice; and the attempts of the father and sons to satisfy this desire.

It thus is unsurprising that when I asked the Koa children to describe the good guys in *Swiss Family Robinson*, they often answered "the family." It is the children's explanations of what they find attractive about the Robinson family that are troubling. Their comments suggest that they bring to the film relentlessly middle-class conceptions about how families look and act. In their discussions of good guys and bad guys in *Swiss Family Robinson*, the Koa students' normative notions of the family exist alongside a companion discourse about the deviance and dangerousness of poor people and of men who live outside of families.

As I've argued in previous chapters, it is important to keep in mind that the fact that in focus group discussions of a Hollywood film children reproduce dominant ideological positions doesn't necessarily mean that they endorse these positions in real life. Nevertheless, I worry more about the Koa students' ability to question the class messages in *Swiss Family Robinson* than I do about their ability to resist the film's violence, sexism, racism, and colonialism. Class prejudice in American society is a problem that is less visible and more intractable than racial prejudice. American courts have mandated measures to achieve the racial integration of schools but show little inclination to address social class segregation. Children get much less help from the curriculum in seeing what's wrong with class than with racial prejudice. School libraries these days have many books about families from diverse cultural, racial, and regional backgrounds, but few books about contemporary families who are poor (*A Christmas Carol* and some of the *Little House on the Prairie* books depict impoverished families, but in a sentimentalized past rather than a threatening present). In children's movies with poor or working-class protagonists, the plotline is nearly always a twist on the Horatio Alger saga of unfettered social mobility, where within the time frame of the movie characters such as Aladdin and Cinderella rise dramatically from a deprived past to a fantastically wealthy future. Such narratives reinforce rather than disrupt the stability of class privilege.

Ideas about class cannot easily be separated from ideas about gender. The family is where class and gender meet. What distinguishes the middle class from the poor below and the rich above is not just income and education, but also norms of masculinity and femininity. The Koa students' discussion of what makes the Robinsons attractive and the pirates despicable reflects a confluence of ideas about class and gender. Four core characteristics of the Robinson family's goodness came up repeatedly in the focus group discussions: domesticity, niceness, industriousness, and a married-with-children version of masculinity.

DOMESTICITY

In the passage quoted at the beginning of this chapter, what did Lia mean when she said that "The good guys were all staying in their place"? The phrase is confusing, because to "stay in one's place" sounds to adult ears a bit like "to know one's place." This is one possible meaning—the Robinsons know and occupy their appropriate class location, in contrast to the pirates, who, not knowing or accepting their place in the world, are attempting to take someone else's. The pirates coming up from below to attack the Robinsons thus can be read not only, as suggested in the previous chapter, as an allegory for their attempt to climb colonialism's evolutionary ladder, but also as a dastardly attempt to jump social class barriers. This notion of the middle-class family as needing to defend its class position and possessions from the predatory desires of the lower classes is a powerful trope in Hawai'i, as it is in many other American localities. For example, at a recent conference I attended in Honolulu, a political scientist suggested that one alternative scenario for Hawai'i in the next decade is "high walls, big dogs." By this he meant that middle-class families in Hawai'i might move in ever-increasing numbers into gated communities designed to keep the poor outside and at bay. "High walls, big dogs" is also a pretty good description of the scene from *Swiss Family Robinson* I showed the children at Koa. The Robinsons erect high walls and use their big dogs (and other weapons) to repel the pirates (see Figure 6.1). Most of the children at Koa come from families who cannot afford to live in fully gated and guarded communities. But many live in townhouse complexes that include such security precautions as surveillance cameras, tire spikes, and pass cards. The scenario depicted in the movie, of a nice middle-class family staying in their place and defending it against criminals, thus has considerable resonance with the real life experience of many Koa children, whose parents install car and house alarms and stress the importance of locking doors and being wary of strangers encountered on the streets between the middle-class domestic enclosures of home and school.

Another possible meaning of "the good guys were all staying in their place" is that what makes the good guys in the movie good is their domesticity and what makes the bad guys bad is their nomadic homelessness. Lia was not alone in making such a suggestion. Similar comments include "The good guys were the family inside the house and the bad guys were the ones outside," "One team was defending their house and the other team was attacking," and "The family made a real nice house with ropes and stuff and the bad guys wanted it." The children's attraction to things that are nice and domestic seems relatively innocent and unproblematic until we consider that the flip side may be a demonizing of people who lack nice things and don't have homes. If people who have nice places and stay in them are the good guys, it follows that people who don't have nice places to stay are marked as bad and dangerous.

The pirates in *Swiss Family Robinson* were bad guys who posed a real threat to the Robinsons. Thus the fact that the children at Koa identified the pirates as evil and dangerous is not in itself surprising or disturbing. What is

Figure 6.1. The coconut-toting boy is in a cozy, symmetrical enclosure. Although the scene the children watched showed the family outside, fighting from behind rocks and stone barricades, in many of their comments and drawings the children suggest that the good guys were inside a domestic enclosure.

disturbing is the possibility that watching *Swiss Family Robinson* may work to strengthen a preexisting tendency in some children to believe that people who are poor and homeless are deficient and dangerous. Homelessness is a controversial and politicized issue in Hawai'i. On the one hand, there is sympathy at Koa, particularly among the students and teachers in the Hawaiian-language immersion program, for the homeless Hawaiians who construct tent communities on the beaches and fight efforts of the state and federal governments to dislodge them. Homelessness in this context is given a human face and a historical cause, as it is connected to the colonizers' dispossession of the Hawaiians from the land (Kame'eleihiwa, 1992). On the other hand, the children at Koa cannot help but share in the popular perception, supported by broadcast news stories, that many crimes are committed by homeless people.

In classroom discussions of homelessness and of political events such as Hawaiian sovereignty activist Bumpy Kanahele's arrest for establishing a tent city at Makapu'u Beach, I've heard children at Koa express compassion for homeless children, sympathy for people who have been dispossessed from the land, and an appreciation of the complexity of the causes of poverty and homelessness. However, none of this compassion, sympathy, or complexity came out in the discussions of the good guys and bad guys in *Swiss Family Robinson*. I suspect this is because the movie presents the pirates' villainy and nomadic lifestyle and the Robinsons' goodness and domesticity in such black-and-white terms that there is little opportunity to introduce a counterdiscourse. But at least on these issues of homelessness and property, counterdiscourses circulate in the Koa community.

NICENESS

In the focus group discussions, students described the good guys as "the ones wearing the nice clothes," "the people with nice faces," and "the family in the nice house." One girl referred to the Robinsons as "the nice family who got attacked." It's clear that children at Koa believe that at least in movies, good guys are people who are nice and who have nice things. What is not so clear is what, exactly, they mean by "nice."

Nice is a slippery signifier. "Nice" appears 22 times in my interview transcripts, used to mean either "kind" (the mom in the Cheerios commercial "is a real nice mom"), "attractive" ("nice clothes," "nice house"), or something in between ("the ones with nice faces"). What is the central meaning of "nice" that allows this word to be used by the children at Koa to describe both people and their possessions? For a synonym that would cover all their usages of the word, I suggest we consider "middle-class."

Children at Koa lack a precise vocabulary for talking about class. This is hardly surprising, considering that Americans in general lack such a vocabulary. In Great Britain, class conflict and class distinctions are part of everyday discourse in the popular media, in politics, in academic scholarship, and even in the curriculum (especially in media studies) in a way that they are not in the United States. Talking and writing about class distinctions in the United States is so rare that we often feel the need to add the word "social" to indicate that we are talking about a stratified system of privileges and status, not about a school classroom. Americans like to believe that this is so because (social) class is relatively unimportant in the United States, a nation that congratulates itself on its class mobility and lack of snobbery. I disagree.

Although the children at Koa never used the word "class" in the focus group discussions, they seem to have a clear understanding of what it means to be middle-class, and they employ this understanding to distinguish between the good guys and the bad guys in *Swiss Family Robinson*. When they say that the Robinsons look nice and act nice, what they are describing is the family's middle-classness. In this movie, made in 1960 but set in the early 19th century, the Robinson family displays the tastes and style of the middle-class American family of 1960s sitcoms. The children at Koa have no difficulty reading the semiotics of middle-class niceness, which apparently have changed very little since the 1960s. A nice shirt is a shirt that is clean, nontattered, buttoned up, and tucked in. A nice face is one that is well scrubbed, without facial hair, prominent earrings, or an outlandish hairstyle. A nice house (including a nice treehouse) is one with running water, efficient appliances, and separate bedrooms for adults, for boys, and for girls. A nice girl is a girl who must be defended from pirates and other predatory males, but who can flirt with nice boys. And, as we will see, a nice man is a man who lives in a house with his family, whom he defends against people who are not nice.

Niceness is as much about gender as class. Parents and teachers use the word to control young children of both sexes ("If you can't play nicely with the blocks, we're going to have to put them away"). But nice is used much more frequently to pressure girls than boys to be nonaggressive, obliging, and modest in their desires. One of the tensions of middle-class gender expectations is that if boys are too nice in their dress or manner they risk being thought insufficiently masculine. Thus, by the time boys get to be 7 or 8 years old, middle-class adults tend to stop using the word *nice* to praise them. The situation is very different for girls, for whom "niceness" is a socially desirable gender as well as class goal. "Sugar and spice and everything nice," that's still what middle-class little girls are supposed to be made of.

When asked to explain how they identify the bad guys, many of the children answered by referring to the pirates' dirty, unkempt, and generally unappealing appearance: "They were dirty and they tried to invade the place where the family was," "Their pants, they didn't come all the way down like regular pants does, and they were like all torn up on the bottom," "Because they had clothes on that's like junk," and "They looked ugly and they had missing teeth, missing front teeth, and they had swords."

I think what the children are picking up on here is how the semiotics of class as well as race and colonialism are deployed in the film to mark the pirates as evil and the Robinsons as good. Adventure movies in general and children's adventure movies in particular are overwritten, to make who is good and who is evil abundantly clear to even the most naive viewers. Following this Hollywood logic of redundant signifiers, it is not enough to make the bad guys pirates; they must also be dark-skinned, bare-chested, grunting, dirty, disheveled, stupid, clumsy, and with hair and dental problems. Just as the Robinson family is nice in countenance as well as in character and tastes, so the pirates are mean both in the contemporary sense of being cruel and in the older sense of being low-class and poor. It's clear that the children at Koa know how to read this grammar of niceness, meanness, and class. What's not clear is the degree to which they apply this grammar to their judgments of goodness and badness in real life.

INDUSTRIOUSNESS AND INGENUITY

Children in many of the focus groups suggested that the family's industriousness marks them as the good guys in the film. The equation of hard work with middle-class status may seem paradoxical in that presumably one of the main motivations for obtaining a white-collar job is the opportunity to escape sweaty, dangerous, body-aching labor. A key mystification of the class system is the suggestion that middle-class managers work harder than the wage laborers they supervise. Middle-class workers may not literally bleed and sweat, but they nevertheless claim to pour their blood and sweat into their businesses. One of the most significant ideological inventions of the 18th century is the notion of the goodness and value of middle-class labor. Daniel Defoe's *Robinson Crusoe* (1719) played a significant role in the development of this new notion of work by depicting the ability of one intelligent, educated, industrious middle-class man to transform an undeveloped environment. It is Crusoe's ingenuity, technological know-how, and diligence more than his physical strength that allow him to live successfully on his tropical island. When Johann David Wyss wrote *Swiss Family Robinson* in 1811, he echoed not just Robinson Crusoe's plot but also its celebration of the goodness of middle-class industriousness and ingenuity. Dorfman (1983) points out that many children's stories, including the Babar books and Disney's Donald Duck comics, share with the various versions of the Robinson Crusoe story the "reduplication of the entire successful and frugal history of the birth of a managerial class" (p. 33).

Disney's *Swiss Family Robinson* film endorses the same values, as it includes many scenes of the family as a whole, and the father in particular, working. The work depicted in the film is often physically strenuous, but it rises above brute labor in that it is always carefully planned, clever, and technologically sophisticated (see Figure 6.2). Much of the Robinsons' labor is invested in building labor-saving devices, including a system to provide running water to the house and an elephant-powered elevator.

The Koa children find the Robinsons' middle-class approach to work very attractive. For instance, Kevin, age 11, praised the Robinsons' inventiveness: "They're smart, the good guys, and the bad guys aren't smart. The good guys made rope. They didn't buy it. They made it themselves with the coconut things." Nicole, age 8, appreciated the hours of preparation the Robinsons invested in defending themselves: "It must have taken a long time to make so many traps." Terry, age 10, enthusiastically described how the family built their treehouse:

The other part of the movie we didn't see is really cool. I've got the tape at home. I've watched it a million times. You should see the part when they make an elevator thing in the treehouse. They use a baby elephant. The elephant is the motor and it goes up and down! And they make a water thing for doing the dishes up in the treehouse and everything.

Dorfman (1983) points out that ingenuity is a key marker of civilization and goodness in colonialist children's works: "In all these, and so many other twentieth-century products, having a 'brilliant idea' is not only what allows a contestant to win in the game of life. It is also a sign that such a victory is well deserved" (p. 35).

I suggested above that the children at Koa see the Robinsons' cleanliness as a sign of their goodness and the pirates' dirtiness as a sign that they are evil. What, then, are we to make of 8-year-old Sophia's discussion of the good guys and bad guys?

INTERVIEWER: Did the good guys and the bad guys look different?
SOPHIA: Yeah, they had different costumes and different faces.
INTERVIEWER: How were their faces different?
SOPHIA: One was dirty and one wasn't.
INTERVIEWER: Who had the dirty faces?
SOPHIA: The father, who threw the things down the hill.

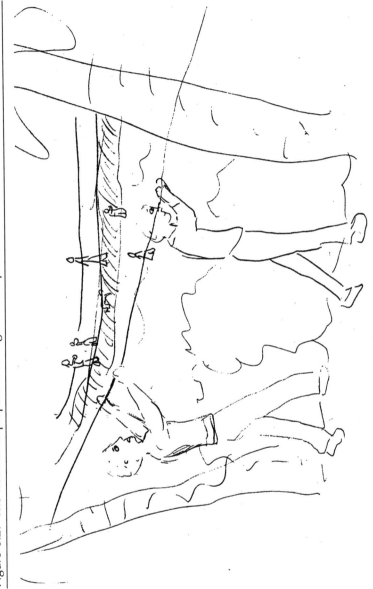

Figure 6.2. The Robinsons prepare their ingenious traps.

Sophia's comment doesn't make much sense until we go back to the *Swiss Family Robinson* video and look closely at the moment she is describing. The father doesn't actually throw anything, but he does chop through a rope, thereby unleashing an avalanche of logs (see Figure 6.3). As the logs roll down the hill, conking the pirates on the head and halting their attack, the film cuts to a shot of the father, who gives a slight smile of relief as he sees that his planning and hard work have paid off. In this close-up shot we see beads of perspiration on John Mills's brow, which he wipes away with his handkerchief. I think that when Sophia describes the father as having a dirty face, she is referring to this sweaty brow. Her use of the word "dirty" to mean "sweaty" reflects a linguistic and cognitive confusion about body functions that, in my experience, is not uncommon in 6-year-olds. Deodorant commercials on television, a staple of middle-class American consumer society, contribute to the confusion of sweat with dirt by dramatizing the horror of being seen in public in perspiration-stained clothes. Sophia's approval of Father Robinson's sweatiness suggests that she understands the dignity of hard work. Her referring to his sweatiness as dirtiness suggests that she is already caught up in the middle-class notion that middle-class bodies are not supposed to sweat. Thus what looks at first like idiosyncratic confusion can be more usefully understood as Sophia's expressing the larger society's contradictory messages about laboring bodies.

The other hallmark of the Robinsons' exemplary middle-class industriousness and ingenuity is their efficient, rational use and control of nature. In several of the groups, children who were familiar with the movie made comments suggesting that the Robinsons' goodness can be located in their stewardship of the land and their animal husbandry: "The family had so little food so they made a nice farm and then they could eat all their own food"; "They saved the animals from the boat so they didn't get drownded"; "There were so many kinds of animals and they took care of all of them and rode them and stuff."

This idea that good guys are people who are industrious and smart and who care for animals is expressed in the following passage by a group of 5- and 6-year olds, although a bit cryptically:

INTERVIEWER: Was that movie real or made up?

KEONI: Made up.

INTERVIEWER: How can you tell?

KEONI: 'Cause if it was real it would be somewhere around the world. Like, it would be somewhere like on earth. But it didn't look like an earth.

INTERVIEWER: It didn't seem like a real place?

KEONI: No.

INTERVIEWER: Where do you think that place was?

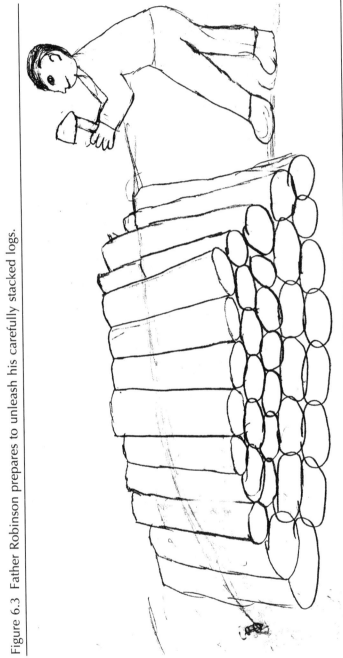

Figure 6.3 Father Robinson prepares to unleash his carefully stacked logs.

DYLAN: Texas?
KENCHIRO: Africa.
ELIJAH: Egypt.
KEONI: Italy.
DYLAN: Italy is shaped like a boot.
INTERVIEWER: Were there good guys and bad guys?
KENCHIRO: Yeah!
INTERVIEWER: Who were the good guys and who were the bad guys?
KEONI: The good guys were in the house.
KENCHIRO: The guys with the beard. Those was bad guys and the good
    guys was on the mountain.
INTERVIEWER: Who were the bad guys?
DYLAN: The ones who was attacking.
ELIJAH: The ones with swords and stuff.
INTERVIEWER: In that short amount of time, how can you tell who is a bad
    guy and who is a good guy?
KEONI: 'Cause the good guys don't have, uh, hats.
ELIJAH: Or weapons.
KENCHIRO: 'Cause the good guys are more smarter than the bad guys.
DYLAN: The bad guys don't have horses or anything.

The non sequitor about Italy being boot-shaped I chalk up to a 6-year-old's associative logic (Cazden, 1987; Newkirk, 1992). Young children have very different notions from adults of what it means to keep a conversation on topic. From the perspective of first-graders' conversational rules, Dylan's comment that "Italy is shaped like a boot" is a perfectly appropriate rejoinder to Keoni's guess that *Swiss Family Robinson* took place in Italy. The comments about hats and horses require deeper analysis before they come to make sense. When I was a child in the 1950s, good guys routinely wore hats—cowboys had their 10-gallon hats, baseball players their caps, soldiers and firemen their helmets, and businessmen their fedoras. But the customs and semiotics of hat-wearing began to change in the 1960s. Keoni is correct in his observation that in the *Swiss Family Robinson* video segment they watched the bad guys wear headgear (bamboo hats, fezzes, Chinese coolie caps, bandanas) while the Robinsons' heads are bare (see Figure 6.4). Keoni's comment also can be understood as citing a contemporary hot issue in schools. Baseball caps are now associated with rap music, gang culture, and disrespect for adult authority, leading some schools, including Koa, to set rules against hat wearing.

Dylan's comment about horses is tough to decipher, as it requires that we follow a chain of inferences. If the bad guys are bad because they don't have horses, that would suggest that the good guys are good because they do

Figure 6.4. Bad guys with hats.

have horses. The Robinsons don't have horses, but they do have many other animals that they harness and ride as one would a horse, including a very large dog, an ostrich, and a baby elephant. I think Dylan has offered an interesting insight here into the association of middle-class values with the keeping of pets and the domesticating of animals. Farm families, who are the original American middle class, care for crops and animals; suburban middle-class families have house pets. It is interesting that Dylan chooses horses as an example of an animal because horses are a complex signifier, with different meanings for different social classes—work animal for the rural working class, sporting animal for the upper classes, and, as we saw in Chapter 3, objects of longing for little girls of the middle class.

BAD GUYS AND GOOD WOMEN

One of the key distinctions the Koa children make between good guys and bad guys in movies is that good guys live with women and bad guys with other men. In group after group, the children were quick to explain that the good guys in *Swiss Family Robinson* were the men in families, the ones in the house, and the ones with the children, and the bad guys the ones who hang out in an all-male horde. The prevailing opinion among the children at Koa is that the categories of bad guys and women are mutually exclusive (see Figure 6.5). The children had difficulty, however, answering our follow-up questions about why bad guys have no women and why women can't be bad guys. Some kids saw no need to provide an explanation other than suggesting that this is just how it is, a fact of life: "Pirates don't have women," "There are no women Indians," and "Ladies can't be bad guys." Others, viewing bad guys as a sort of species or race or tribe, felt that bad guys must have women somewhere or they would be unable to reproduce themselves. They offered as a solution to this conundrum that the bad guys lead a sort of double life, going out with their male horde to commit mayhem and then returning to their campsite or pirate ship, where they are the patriarchs of traditional families with stay-at-home wives:

INTERVIEWER: Did you see any girls that were with the bad guys?
DEREK: No.
INTERVIEWER: Why do you suppose that is?
NOLAN: Cuz Indians don't have girls.
HISAE: I saw some girls.
MARY-JANE: Yes, they have girls. Only some.
NOLAN: Only the boy Indians fight when they go out.
INTERVIEWER: What do you think the girls were doing?

Figure 6.5. Good guys as ladies in dresses and bad guys as men with hats (or turbans). Although the female characters in the movie wore simple dresses, some of the ladies in these drawings wear ball gowns and heels.

DEREK: Staying home.
NOLAN: Taking care of babies.
INTERVIEWER: How come there weren't any bad guys as girls or women?
LANCE: Pirates can be girls, but . . . maybe they were back at the ship?

INTERVIEWER: Did you see any women in the pirate group?
KAHELE: No.
INTERVIEWER: Why was that?
KAHELE: Because the women are precious. The men are the strong ones.
TRAVIS: The men fight and the women, like, I don't know . . .
INTERVIEWER: Casey, do you agree with Kahele?
CASEY (shrugging): 'Cause they would die easily.
INTERVIEWER: So the women just hang out together?
HADRIAN: Sometimes they cook, or be like waitresses.
TRAVIS: I saw a woman on the good guys' team.
INTERVIEWER: Why was that?
HADRIAN: 'Cause that was the guy's friend.
KAHELE: That was the girlfriend, I think.
INTERVIEWER: Did you see any girls in this movie?
STEPHANIE: One. She had a blue dress.
INTERVIEWER: Was she good or bad?
STEPHANIE: Good.
INTERVIEWER: How could you tell?
STEPHANIE: She had a dress on, and the girls wouldn't be wearing a dress if she was bad.
ASHLEY: They wear pants.
INTERVIEWER: There weren't any girl pirates? I wonder why.
ASHLEY: 'Cause men are more stronger than girls.

In these passages, the Koa children's firm belief in traditional gender roles is stated on several levels: Good guys are good because they live in nuclear families, with a patriarchal family structure and clearly prescribed gender roles. Bad guys are bad because they live outside family life, in a world of the male horde. But when the bad guys are done marauding, they go home to their village or ship, where they have middle-class family lives, with their Indian or pirate wives who keep house and cook and take care of children, just like moms on sitcoms.

This story, although told over and over again in the focus-group discussions at Koa, isn't all that stable. It is challenged on the one hand by feminist arguments. In several groups, girls argued back that "Girls can too fight," and that "Girls can be bad guys if they want to be." I think these counterarguments to the prevailing male chauvinism were relatively rare because the girls with feminist beliefs weren't so sure that being able to fight and being capable of being a bad guy were appropriate feminist goals. To argue that girls, too, can play basketball or be engineers or doctors is one thing; to argue that they, too, can be rampaging pirates or marauding Indians on the warpath is quite another. I think another reason girls hesitated to challenge the sexism implicit in the suggestion that women can't be bad guys has to do with their understanding of gender performance and movie genres. We asked the children to tell us how they identify the bad guys in an adventure movie. In adventure movies and horror films, the villains are almost always male. Had we asked the same question about villains in animated movies, I suspect we would have heard a lot about evil stepmothers and witches and fur-wearing puppy killers. Another factor has to do with the terms we used to pose our question. "Bad guys" is strongly gender-biased, in contrast to the British term "baddies."

THE DILEMMA OF MIDDLE-CLASS MASCULINITY

Another point of tension in the Koa children's notion that, at least in movies, good guys live in homes with wives and children and bad guys in groups of men is that they find the bad guys and their lifestyle very attractive. Good guys and bad guys represent contrasting versions of masculinity. The bad-guy version is the more purely masculine, the good-guy version an awkward compromise between masculinity and domesticity. The good-guy version of masculinity, represented in *Swiss Family Robinson* in the character of the father, is a domesticated, oversocialized, desexualized figure.

This is an issue that is portrayed as a stock scene in ordinary westerns and explored in the more thoughtful movies of this genre. A classic scene in the western is that of a settler/farmer being teased for being insufficiently masculine by cowpokes, ranchers, or gunslingers. These scenes are as much about class as gender: the object of the teasing is ridiculed for looking and acting like a middle-class man. I remember the mixed emotions I felt as a child watching these scenes. Seeing a settler getting taunted in a western was much more disturbing than seeing someone in the movie get shot or hung because it was much more real to me—in my daily life, in my school and neighborhood, I knew I was much more likely to be teased, like the farmers and tenderfooted city slickers, than I was to be shot or hung. It was also disturbing because the men being teased so unmercifully in these movies and made to dance around in saloons while bad guys shot near their feet and chased them out of town were men who looked and acted like my dad. In laughing at the tenderfoot, I felt a sense of identifying with the aggressors who teased me at school (the bullies, our version of pirates and gunfighters), and of betraying my father (who, like the settlers in the movie, wore store-bought clothes, worked hard to support us, and lived with us, away from the company of other men). In doing so, I was participating in the denigration of the version of masculinity that even then I knew I was on my way to adopting.

In our imaginary play as children we never chose to be the ranchers, the settlers, the town doctor, the bartender, or the newspaper reporter from back east. We chose to be the sheriff, the gunfighter, the outlaws, or the Indians. It's more exciting to be the Indians, who get to whoop it up, fight with abandon, and shoot actual (rubber-tipped) projectiles than to be the cowboys or settlers, who shoot from behind cover, firing imaginary bullets while they yell, "Bang, I gotcha!". In the Hollywood western, as in children's play, Indians, outlaws, and gunfighters are more compelling figures than the domesticated, middle-class males.

These dynamics are explored in *Shane*, a western that is about our ambivalence toward middle-class masculinity. The little boy in the movie (Little Joe) plays the part of us; the audience. Through his eyes we see the divergent masculinities of the Old West. His comments articulate our longings, our fears, and our deep ambivalence about the workings of class and gender. In *Shane* a homesteader, who is also a husband and father (Joe Starrett, played by Van Heflin), is threatened with being run off his land by Ryker, a rancher, a rough-hewn, arrow-scarred patriarchal tamer of the frontier. The plot—and definitions of masculinity—get more complex when this opposing pair is mirrored by the addition of another opposing pair, the nomadic loner and ex-gunfighter Shane (Alan Ladd), who takes a job as a hired hand on the Starrett homestead, and the sinister gunfighter Wilson (Jack Palance), who is employed by Ryker to chase off the homesteaders. A third opposing pair of minor characters provide additional variants of masculinity: Calloway (Ben Johnson), Ryker's ranch hand, teases and goads Shane, whom he mistakes for a tenderfoot. Torrey (Elisha Cook) is a hot-headed homesteader and Confederate Army veteran. The tensions between these pairs of men are played out in predictable Hollywood fashion: in shootouts, Wilson kills Torrey, then Shane kills Wilson and Ryker. What is extraordinary in this film is the dialogue and glances exchanged between Little Joe, his mother, father, and Shane. It becomes embarrassingly clear to the characters in the movie and to us that not only does Little Joe prefer Shane's undomesticated masculinity to his father's domesticated version, but that his mother feels the same way. Poignantly, even Big Joe doesn't blame his son or wife for preferring Shane. Each member of the family admits in various ways that he or she is deeply excited by Shane's masculinity (symbolized by his skill with guns) and that Big Joe's death would seem to provide a desired solution to their dilemma. But Shane knows that he must make room for the civilized, domestic, middle-class men, including both Joe Starretts, who will take his place in the developing American society. It is clear to Shane, if not to the Starrett family, that his sexualized, violent, hair-trigger version of masculinity, which is ideally suited to showdowns with bad guys and to winning the hearts of little boys and their mothers, would be inappropriate and unsuccessful if brought within the domestic confines of farming, town life, and the nuclear family.

These competing versions of masculinity are on display in *Swiss Family Robinson*. The children at Koa are intrigued and excited by the undomesticated masculinity of the pirates. These savage men are made to look more ridiculous than menacing in the movie, but the children nevertheless are drawn to their swagger, exotic clothing, weapons, and freedom from the demands of civilization. Father Robinson is an attractive but problematic model of masculinity. He is brave and strong, but living as he does among women and children and farm animals, he is too socialized and domesticated to be an appealing object for either desire or identification. The movie provides more attractive masculine figures in the characters of the three Robinson boys. Jack, the youngest, who throws the coconut bombs, is the Koa children's great favorite. He is a member of a middle-class family, but because he is young, he is given considerable leeway by his parents (and the script) to be a bit naughty and reckless. He may be destined for boring, middle-class masculinity, but he's not there yet. The two older boys, Fritz and Ernst, resemble Shane more than Joe Starrett. Unlike their father, who displays no strong emotions or desires, the teenage boys are daring, reckless, hot-headed, and lustful. We are reminded in the script that they are on their way to mundane middle-class lives (the movie concludes with Fritz being packed off to medical school and Ernst betrothed to the captain's daughter). But within the main action of the movie they are allowed to fight, dress, and lust like, well, savages (for such is the link in our cultural imagination between the adolescent and the primitive).

The story of masculinity and class thus is further complicated by life stage. The children at Koa find Jack, Fritz, and Ernst Robinson attractive because these characters, like Shane, are good guys who are not yet fully domesticated. They are linked to families and homes, but they spend most of their time outside the domestic enclosure (exploring, hunting, and riding the animals). In this regard, the boys in the movie are like schoolchildren, who live in families but hang out during the day as much as they can with members of their own sex. In movies as in real life, men and boys in groups away from women are highly ambivalent signifiers. As soldiers, athletes, and cowboys, they are idealized male figures whom children are encouraged to imitate in socially sanctioned activities including imaginary play, Boy Scouts, and youth sports. But as members of drug cartels, youth gangs, and the urban underclass, young men in groups are feared and loathed.

Middle-class American culture resolves this ambivalence in part by seeing male homosociality as something that is supposed to wind down in late childhood or early adolescence. In fact, this notion that homosociality is primarily a stage of the life cycle is a hallmark of the middle class. Aristocratic men have their all-male clubs and working-class men their bars and bowling leagues. But middle-class men are expected to put their relationships with their wives and children ahead of hanging out with their pals and, like Father Robinson, to be satisfied with a life of family domesticity. As a kind of safety valve, middle-class men are allowed to have episodes (as in *City Slickers*) when they are allowed to retreat from the rigors of relating to women and children and to regress, temporarily, to the primitive joys of male bonding.

Koa is a community that straddles the divide separating the middle from the working class. Middle-class families at Koa struggle, and sometimes fail, to maintain a middle-class lifestyle. A handful of the better-off children will attend private schools after Koa Elementary School, but most Koa graduates are on their way to a middle school nearby that is known to have gang activity. The link between male homosociality and violence is frightening but also exciting to the children at Koa. The principal and counselor at Koa, aware of the allure gangs hold for preadolescents like those at Koa, periodically invite policemen, high school anti-drug clubs, and other inspirational speakers to visit the school to implore the students to "Do the right thing" and "Just say no to gangs and drugs." The older students at Koa seem to be attracted to the masculine coolness of youth gangs but afraid of and repulsed by the violence.

THE DANGER OF WOMANLESS, CHILDLESS MEN

Given the complexity of our society's attitudes toward masculinity, it is to be expected that the children at Koa would have conflicted feelings about the range of male characters in *Swiss Family Robinson*. They know that the father is the ideal male character in the film, but they find the pirates and the not yet fully domesticated boys much more attractive and exciting. I think these reactions are inevitable and benign. I also am not terribly concerned about the film's unreconstructed male chauvinism because I find that the children at Koa bring effective counterdiscourses to discussions of gender equity issues. The lingering worry I have about the Koa children's engagement with gender and class issues in *Swiss Family Robinson* is that I read in their enjoyment and apparent acceptance of the film's presentations of masculinity a fear of men who are not aligned with middle-class families.

In group after group, children at Koa described the bad guys as the men without homes, nice clothes, good grooming, and women and children. I find this worrisome on several counts—first, because it suggests a belief, which Disney and other filmmakers tap into, that poor people are dangerous to middle-class families; second, because it encourages fear and loathing for the homeless, who tend to be portrayed in the news as hordes of men without women and children; and third, because in the equation of womanless and childless men with danger, I perceive the workings of homophobia. Bad guys in Disney animated films are often effeminate (I'm thinking, for example, of the vanity and prissiness of Captain Hook in *Peter Pan*, Gaston in *Beauty and the Beast*, Jafar in *Aladdin*, Governor Ratcliffe in *Pocahontas*, and Scar in *The Lion King*). In *Swiss Family Robinson*, while the pirate horde are swarthy and rough-clad, the Pirate Chief is feminized by his pencil mustache, hoop earring, scarf, and extravagant eye makeup. Effeminacy aside, the suggestion that men who don't live in families are dangerous to children is a pernicious fiction in the morally panicked, homophobic era in which we live (Tobin, 1997). Koa is a relatively liberal, sensible place when it comes to questions of equity and social justice. But at Koa, as at most early childhood educational settings in America, male teachers (especially if they are unmarried) work under a cloud of suspicion. Movies such as *Swiss Family Robinson*, *Hook*, and *Home Alone*, which have as their villains unmarried men who want to do harm to children, are ideologically dangerous because they add fuel to homophobic panics that already are burning nearly out of control.

This theme of men outside of families posing dangers to children came up in many of the discussions, but most explicitly in the comments of a group of 6- and 7-year-old girls who made an associative, intertextual leap from *Swiss Family Robinson* to *Peter Pan* and the sequel, *Hook*:

INTERVIEWER: Were there good guys and bad guys?
SOPHIA: Yeah.
SADE: The good guys were the ones throwing coconut bombs.
ASHLEY: And the bad guys was those pirates.
MARY-ANN: Those Japanese people.
INTERVIEWER: How did you know they were the bad guys?
ASHLEY: Because they were pirates. Like in *Hook* . . .
SADE: They were trying to take over the land.
MELISSA: And they had bad guys and good guys.
INTERVIEWER: And who were the bad guys in *Hook*?
ASHLEY: Hook.
INTERVIEWER: And he was a . . .
SADE: Pirate.
MELISSA: He stole Peter's children.
ASHLEY: Oh, I know that. But that wasn't his children.
MELISSA: Yes, it was!
ASHLEY: But he's not even married.
MELISSA: How do you think he had kids?

SADE: If there's a pirate, there must be a good guy.
SOPHIA: I wonder how they make coconut bombs. Maybe they just drew
    them.

In this passage, the threats posed to children by men of ambiguous sexuality
are ominous and ill-defined. Peter, the elflike boy who won't grow up and
who is usually performed on stage by a woman, and Hook, the vain, whining
pirate who has been symbolically castrated by the crocodile, are both presented in this discussion as having peculiar interests in children. The girls
agree that Hook, like the pirates in *Swiss Family Robinson*, wants to steal the
children. But they are confused by the nature of Peter's interest in the children, who, they reason, can't be his because he isn't married. (Michael Jack-
son naming his estate "Neverland" only adds to the confusion.)

The flip side to this belief in the danger posed to children by unmarried
men is the safety children expect to enjoy in middle-class families. The reality
is that very few sexual abusers of children are gay men, or men living alone.
The majority are married men or other family members who live in the same
household or belong to the same extended family as the victim. The belief of
the children at Koa that the people who are most dangerous to them are
anonymous men who are gay, poor, or both and that families are safe havens
is therefore not only factually wrong but pathetic, as we can see in the comments of three 10-year-old girls:

KAUMEALOHA: I hate those pirate guys. They look so mean and ugly and
    they're coming up and attacking the family who didn't even do any-
    thing to them and they're just defending themselves.
JOCELYN: Me too. I hate the pirates too, cuz in the real movie, they was try-
    ing to take that girl, you know that one who had clothes on like a boy,
    to take her away from the Robinsons.
SHAREEN: I like the good guys, the nice family, cuz if it was real life they
    would help us and protect us if someone was trying to hurt us.

There are strong counterdiscourses that children at Koa can draw on to
resist sexism, racism, and colonialism in movies, but I fear that the class
bias and homophobia, connecting as they do with preexisting anxieties and
prejudices, embedded in movies such as *Swiss Family Robinson* are more
difficult for the children at Koa to resist. The idealization of the middle-
class family as a safe haven from sexual and other kinds of abuse and the
accompanying projection of society's fears about the vulnerability of children
onto single men, the homeless, African Americans, and the poor are a pernicious mystification that protects no one from harm while contributing to our
society's racial and class divisions and general mean-spiritedness.

CHAPTER 7

Conclusion

This book has turned out to be about several things: not just children's understandings of media representations of violence, gender, race, colonialism, and
class, but also about children's talk, and innovative approaches to making
sense of their talk. In the preceding chapters, my discussion of these issues
has been closely tied to one setting and one text. In this concluding chapter,
I will shift from Koa Elementary School and *Swiss Family Robinson* to less
contextualized speculations on media effects, children's talk, and interpretive
methods.

THE DETECTIVE AND THE PSYCHOANALYST

In each of the chapters of this book, I've set out a concern about children and
the media, presented transcripts of children's conversations, and then offered
interpretations. The elements of each chapter are similar to those of the detective story and the psychoanalytic case study: a cast of characters and a setting;
a problem (a crime, a neurosis, a puzzling statement made by a child); and
an investigator who gives order to the proceedings by establishing and then
systematically analyzing a cryptic text. In the detective story, this text is made
up of the clues left at the crime scene and eyewitness reports. In psychoanalysis, the text is composed of symptoms, slips, associations, and dreams. In this
book, the texts are transcripts of focus group conversations in which children
say things about *Swiss Family Robinson* that are ambiguous, contradictory,
disturbing, or odd. Because the transcripts I've presented here, like the clues
in a mystery or the symptoms in a case study, are at first indecipherable (or
deceptively transparent), the reader experiences a tension that mirrors the tension of the investigator. This tension is not a bad thing. It is a precursor and
prerequisite to the pleasure we experience when meaning eventually emerges.
Each time I've started on a new piece of dialogue from a focus group discussion, I've felt a sense of excitement mixed with apprehension. On the one
hand, I've felt optimistic that meaning would emerge even when dealing with

the most banal and confusing of transcripts. On the other hand, I've experienced a sense of worry or even temporary despair: "*This* transcript really does lack meaning. I won't be able to make anything out of this one. What the kids are saying here is trivial, silly, banal, vapid, indecipherable." And yet for me as a researcher and writer and, I hope, for you as a reader, with transcript after transcript, line after line, the children's statements eventually have yielded meaning, allowing us to discover anew the acumen children bring to the analysis of media texts and the wit and inexhaustible richness of their talk. This, for me, is the most important point of the book—there is much more meaning in children's talk than we give them credit for, and this meaning can be uncovered if we are sufficiently diligent and imaginative in our approach.

INTERPRETATION AS AN OBSESSIVE ACT

By the standards of social science research, I have invested an extraordinary amount of time and energy working on comments a group of children made in discussions 6 years ago. This book is composed of lengthy analyses of segments of children's talk about a three-minute scene from a video. If my approach seems extreme or obsessive, I suggest it is because researchers in the social sciences are caught up in an economy of efficiency and productivity that compels them to plow through data and research subjects.

Why the rush? Why not take the time to pursue an issue doggedly, considering it from every possible angle? Why not go over a text with a fine-toothed comb, teasing out multiple meanings? Why not take as much time as we need to make sense of statements such as Derek's that the pirates in *Swiss Family Robinson* are Indians, Sophia's that the father had a dirty face, or Lacey's that you can identify the bad guys by their Chinese eyes?

One reason it seems odd to work as long or as intently on a bit of children's conversation as we would, say, on a section of the Dead Sea Scrolls or a poem by Shakespeare is that there is a sense of infinitude about children's talk—if you get stuck deciphering the meaning of a piece of conversation, you can give up and try your hand with the next one. In teaching, parenting, and research, adults have a tendency not to give much attention to any one thing children say because they say so much. Historians of ancient religions and literary scholars obsess over the meanings of small portions of text in part because that is all they have to work with—some have to make a few bits of scroll, a handful of sonnets, or Jane Austen's six novels last them a professional lifetime. They are fortunate, in a way, to have a finite set of material to analyze because if they had more, they might become like social scientists and not try so hard or so carefully to make sense of the texts at their disposal. In this book, I've tried to approach children's conversations about *Swiss Family Robinson* with the kind of respect and assumption of meaning that scholars in the humanities bring to their studies of canonical texts.

I admire the work of researchers who listen carefully to children. Vivian Paley (1981, 1984, 1991), Thomas Newkirk (1988, 1992), Peggy Miller (1982; Miller, et al., 1993), and Cindy Dell Clark (1995), for example, are among the researchers who take what children say seriously. In media studies, Julian Sefton-Green (1993), David Buckingham (1993, 1996) and Ann Haas Dyson (1997) are exemplary in the care they bring to the analysis of transcripts of children talking and writing about popular culture. But as much as I respect and build on the work of these scholars, I believe we can and should dig deeper into the meaning of children's talk and use tools of analysis that are simultaneously more imaginative and systematic.

Reading the work of researchers who interview children about their television-watching, I'm struck by the lucidity of their child informants and left wondering why my informants say so many things that, at least at first, make so little sense. I think the explanation lies in differences in our criteria for selecting segments of interview transcripts to analyze. Focus group studies of children produce hundreds of pages of transcripts. Turning these transcripts into a publication requires an aggressive culling process. Most media researchers select statements from their transcripts that make sense and pass over those that are odd or incoherent. In contrast, I have focused on those moments in my transcripts that I find the most odd, incoherent, and uncanny. In this way, my approach is similar to books such as Paley's *Bad Guys Don't Have Birthdays* (1991) and Dyson's *Writing Superheroes* (1997), in which young children are quoted saying many odd and at first incomprehensible things. But I differ a good deal from Paley and a bit from Dyson in my use of literary and poststructural methods of textual analysis and in my willingness to entertain more speculative interpretations and to offer multiple readings.

ON READING IN

The risk of offering speculative interpretations is that I can be accused of having read meanings that aren't there into the children's words. In any study, there is the danger of researchers projecting their own meanings onto their informants. This is an issue not just in research but also in psychoanalysis, teaching, and indeed in interpersonal relationships in general. To understand another human being, we must use intuition, empathy, and imagination. To make meaning of any statement—spoken, written, or painted—we must read it. And to read is necessarily to read in, for meaning-making is a process not just of decoding but also of interpreting. Making meaning of children's utterances about the media therefore requires us to respond intuitively, imaginatively, and generously to their words. To make sense of the transcripts from Koa Elementary School, I've read something of myself and what I know of the world into the children's talk. To do so is to treat children's speech with the care, dignity, and benefit of doubt we accord the works of poets and scholars.

The concern that I have read something that shouldn't be there into the children's words reflects in part the unfortunate domination of the logic of social science in the fields of media studies and educational research. Social scientists, modeling themselves on the image of hard scientists such as chemists, physicists, and medical researchers, emphasize data analysis over textual interpretation. I suggest, in contrast, that we should think of the task of making sense of our informants' words less as a process of (social) scientific analysis and verification and more as a process akin to literary studies and psychoanalytic interpretation.

Interpreting children's talk has much in common with interpreting a painting, a piece of music, or a literary work. Like works of art, transcripts of children's talk are texts that invite speculative interpretation. These texts can be understood only by a process that includes an act of imagination. If some of my readings of children at Koa talking about *Swiss Family Robinson* are speculative, where's the harm? There is much to gain and little to lose in considering a wide range of interpretations. My goal has not been to sell you on my arguments or to pressure you to agree, but to invite you to join me in a conversation about richly ambiguous texts, such as we might have over coffee after watching an avant-garde film. In the course of such a conversation, if we were to uncover some hidden meanings in the film, we would credit the director for having put them there. Shouldn't we similarly give children credit for having created (if not consciously intended) the hidden meanings we discover in their talk? Why not read them generously?

I can clarify the distinction I make between reading generously and reading fancifully by citing two examples of statements by Clem, whom we met in Chapter 3. When Clem, in the course of his ongoing argument with Shirley, says, "I'm not gonna be no black stallion," I give him credit for having made, however unconsciously, an intertextual allusion to the linking in our culture of sex and race, as embodied in the figures of the black slave in history and the black actor in Hollywood. I feel this reading is justified because it is consistent with other, less obscure statements about racial and sexual politics that Clem makes elsewhere in the interview ("I don't care for the cavalry. It isn't good because the White people . . . I like the Indians"). In contrast, as he watches the moment in *Swiss Family Robinson* when some pirates fall into a tiger pit and says to no one in particular, "Tiger, tiger," it occurs to me that he might be citing William Blake's well-known poem "The Tyger," but I leave this interpretation out of my discussion because it doesn't lead anywhere. Perhaps Clem knows the poem and is referring to it, or perhaps his repetition of the word "tiger" is just a coincidence, but either way it isn't very interesting because I don't see how it helps us make sense of Clem as a media viewer or of Koa Elementary School as a discourse community.

Like interpretations of a patient's talk in a psychoanalytic session, interpretations of children's talk in a research context should work to advance the process of understanding. Psychoanalytic interpretations arise out of the context of the therapeutic encounter, where they are used strategically to further and deepen the dialogic search to uncover unconscious meaning. My interpretations of children's talk about the media are intended to serve a similar function. I took on this project because I felt that as a society we are stuck on the question of how movies affect children. One way to get unstuck, in media research as in psychoanalysis, is for the researcher or analyst to offer provocative interpretations. I hope my readings of children's talk about *Swiss Family Robinson* will have the effect of pushing readers to answer me by coming up with counterinterpretations and thereby to further unstick the debate.

THE RESEARCH CONTEXT

In his essay "Discourse in Life and Discourse in Art" (1926/1976a), Voloshinov argues that the meaning of an utterance can only be understood in context. To understand an utterance we need to attend not only to the words spoken but also to the context, by which he means all that was seen, felt, assumed, and known by the speakers in the conversation. Voloshinov gives the example of two men sitting in a room. One looks out the window and says, "Well." This utterance makes sense only when we know the context: It is autumn, in Russia. From where they are sitting, both men can see out the window. Snow is starting to fall. The men share the experience of having suffered through many long Russian winters. When we understand the context, the simple utterance "Well" has a readily apprehensible meaning. To make sense of an interview transcript, we must retrospectively attempt to recover as much as we can of the context and of what Bakhtin refers to as the speakers' *axiological horizons*. This need for context makes understanding a focus group conversation a difficult but not impossible task.

I discussed contextual features of the setting in the introduction to this book, where I described Koa Elementary School and the larger Pearl City community. Within each chapter, as I've analyzed segments of transcript, I've included contextual information such as the age, gender, and, where it seemed to me to be germane, ethnicities of the children in the focus groups. To explain utterances in the transcripts, I've also provided information about local events and texts to which I believe the children were implicitly referring—University of Hawai'i football games, mean substitute teachers, hotly contested election campaigns, recently released films and video games. As a member of the Koa school community, I had insider knowledge I could bring to my analysis of the children's talk. As an adult member of this community, there was undoubtedly much going on in the children's world of which I was unaware. For each contextual reference I caught, I'm certain there is another that I missed. Even after poring over the transcripts, I still don't get all of the children's local references, in-jokes, and intertextual associations. Such is the reality of making sense of other people's words, in everyday life as well as in research. Had I expanded my research by, for example, listening in on the children's conversations not just at school but also at home, or by interviewing their families, or by conducting individual interviews with each child, I undoubtedly could have made sense of more of the statements they made in the focus groups. But in real life as in research settings, we never can comprehend all of the intertextual associations, concerns, and allusions participants bring to a speech context. Our understandings of utterances therefore are always partial.

One important dimension of the context of the children's utterances in this study is the focus group research format. By choosing to use focus groups, as opposed, for instance, to conducting one-on-one interviews or listening in on children's conversations, I created a specific context that played a key role in the course of the conversations. As a research method, focus group interviews have their advantages and disadvantages. When I teach qualitative research method classes, I give my students a rule of thumb: if your research is on a topic that people commonly discuss with others, do group interviews. Popular media are social texts. A good portion of the pleasure and meaning we get from movies comes from talking about them. Children talk a lot about television and movies at school. Asking them to do so in a focus group interview therefore was asking them to conduct a conversation that I assume is like conversations they have when I'm not present. The showing off, attempting to dominate the conversation, shutting people out, posturing, and so forth that went on in the focus group discussions are similar to the way these children interact in contexts other than a research interview.

On the other hand, it would be ridiculous to suggest that the research context did not have a significant effect on what the children said. I freely grant that the presence of an adult interviewer had much to do with the tone and content of the conversations. To say so is not to admit to a flaw in my research design, but rather to take a necessary interpretive step. The interviewer's presence is a contextual factor that needs to be taken into account to make sense of the children's responses. I prefer focus groups to "listening in" (Newkirk, 1992) on children's spontaneous conversations in part because in a focus group the researcher is explicitly present, which makes researcher effects easier to identify. In focus group settings, it is explicitly the case that the participants are addressing two audiences—their peers in the group and the researcher (and also, less obviously, the audience for the research).

As I look across the transcripts, I see the children alternating between moments when they are explicitly addressing the interviewer (as, for instance, when they respond in the singsong register they reserve for giving insincere answers to teachers and other annoying adults) and moments when they seem largely to ignore the interviewer and to address each other (as, for instance, when Clem was teasing Shirley about her love of horses). I've pointed to instances in several of the transcript segments where I argued that the children were explicitly reacting to or commenting on my research agenda. For example, it is clear to me that the boys in Chapter 2 were aware of what I was up to and what was at stake. They knew that part of my research agenda was to find out if they ever imitate the violent acts they see in movies. They had reason to believe that their answers to my questions could have implications for their freedom to watch violent films in the future. I argued that they also knew a good deal about the media effects debate and that many of their comments can be read as a caricature of this debate ("It's only a movie"; "Get a gun and shoot your friends"). I argued in Chapter 4 that Lacey and Cassidy intuited my research agenda and that their statements about *Swiss Family Robinson* can be interpreted as their playing the parts of the suggestible (Cassidy) and resistant (Lacey) young film viewers of media studies. In this focus group it was particularly clear that the conversation took on the feel of a play, with roles, themes, dramatic tension, theatricality, and plot twists. But the "Chinese eyes" group was by no means the only group that was performing.

In each of the groups, the children and their adult interviewers were performing together, each of us aware of the video camera recording our words and gestures, each of us aware of an audience who would someday watch the tapes and analyze our utterances, each of us aware that in discussions between children and an adult about the media, much (including children's pleasure) is at stake. As discussed in the Introduction, it wasn't always clear who had the upper hand in the interviews. The conversations were ongoing negotiations. As the adult and the researcher, I clearly had the power to direct the conversation and to set the agenda. On the other hand, because my needs were greater in this context than those of the children, they had the power to frustrate me by refusing to answer my questions, by parodying my project, or by answering cryptically. Some of the children, extraordinarily sensitive and savvy, had little trouble reading me. Such sensitivity and savvy are invaluable skills for servants, schoolchildren, and others who must deal all day long with more powerful others. Clever children inferred my agenda and my positions, even when I didn't voice them. In a few cases, the conversations became self-fulfilling prophecies, in which the children, uncannily, said precisely the words I would have scripted for them. "Chinese eyes" was the most uncanny moment in the research for me, because Lacey gave me exactly what I seemed to be looking for at the time—apparent proof that racist movies do indeed interpellate Asian viewers into a self-loathing stance toward their race. But, as I argued in my analysis of this statement in Chapter 4, even in instances where my agenda seemed to dominate the way conversations played out, the children still had the ability to resist my desire to see inside and know them. As in other hierarchical dyads such as teacher/student and employer/employee, the researcher and the researched aren't equal, but that doesn't mean that the less powerful figure in the pair lacks the power to resist, undermine, parody, and in other ways complicate things.

LITERARY AND POSTSTRUCTURAL INTERPRETATION OF CHILDREN'S TALK

Throughout this book I've used tools of literary and critical analysis to make sense of children's unrehearsed conversations. This seems wrong-headed, as speech and writing traditionally have been considered incommensurable phenomena, requiring separate interpretive tools. I've found encouragement for applying literary analysis to transcripts of children's talk in the writings of Bakhtin and his circle. In pointing out the dialogic nature of the novel (1981) and the literariness of speech (1986), Bakhtin suggests that we can analyze both in terms of such rhetorical features as double-voicedness, intertextuality, and citationality. Whether speaking or writing, people communicate by cobbling together a text composed of citations, allusions, and repetitions of the words of others.

I've extended Bakhtinian theory into a research method by tracing out citations, allusions, and intertextual associations in interview transcripts of children's talk. I call this method *Bakhtinian text mapping*. This is the approach I applied in Chapter 2, where I showed that each of the lines of dialogue offered by a group of boys in their discussion of *Swiss Family Robinson* refers, sincerely or parodically, to the debate on media effects and imitative violence.

The appeal for me of this Bakhtinian approach to studying texts harkens back to a childhood memory: I'm watching a television show on which the guest, a linguist, listens to members of the audience talk and then accurately deduces their geographical and social backgrounds. For instance, the linguist says something like, "From the rhythm of your speech and the inflections in your pronunciation, I can tell that you grew up in eastern Nebraska or western Iowa, but one of your parents, probably your mother, came from the South—I would guess the Atlanta area. Your vocabulary suggests that you attended a Catholic college in the Northeast, and you currently work in the legal field." I was enthralled by this performance and remember it (however hazily) to this day because it represented to me not the trickery of a con artist or psychic but instead the potential of a careful, knowledgeable listener to find a great deal of meaning in a few words.

Individuals' utterances reflect not just inflections and vocabulary they've picked up along the way but, more significantly, the worldviews, concerns, and prejudices of the communities in which they've lived. Bakhtinian theory teaches us that the utterances of individuals are most usefully understood as expressions of the perspectives and tensions of their larger society. Because societies are made up of heterogeneous points of view, the speech of individuals necessarily will contain contradictions. Building on this idea, I have taken passages of children talking about *Swiss Family Robinson* and traced out the heterogeneous sources the children cite as they cobble together responses to my questions. I've argued, for example, that the Koa children's understanding of colonialism reflects a combination of such disparate texts as race relations as depicted in Hollywood films, school textbook notions of discovery and Manifest Destiny, sitcom versions of ideal family life, playground rules of justice and fair play, and the National Football League's metaphoric linking of contact sports with combat.

I've been eclectic in my borrowing from literary, philosophical, cultural, gender, and performance theory. In addition to Bakhtin, I've lifted tools of analysis from Jacques Derrida (1976, 1992), Edward Said (1979), Pierre Macherey (1978), Stuart Hall (1991/1997, 1999), Louis Althusser (1972), Michel de Certeau (1984), Michel Foucault (1979), Judith Butler (1990, 1993), and Peggy Phelan (1993). I've used ideas from these authors without taking the time to discuss their work in detail to avoid bogging down my argument in lengthy explications of theory and distracting forays into arcane academic disagreements. I've used various theories to make sense of children's talk rather than using children's talk as an occasion to expound on theory.

Although I have cribbed extensively from poststructural theorists, my approach is not particularly more postmodern than modern, poststructuralist than structuralist, or deconstructive than formalist. Significantly, Bakhtin, the theorist with whom I am most in sympathy, doesn't fit the modern/postmodern binary. My approach to texts is modernist in being earnest and optimistic that with hard work, we can come to find meaning in even the most cryptic and seemingly incoherent of children's statements. It is postmodernist in putting forward multiple meanings and suggesting that we can never be sure that our interpretations are right or that we've gotten to the bottom of things. Some of the techniques I've used to analyze passages of text are modernist/ formalist, such as demonstrating the coherence that can be found from one line to the next spoken by Lacey in the "Chinese eyes" segment. I also have employed poststructuralist techniques, as, for example, in my deconstructive reading of such aporetic statements as Lacey's "They're wasting wood, you should use it as paper."

Derrida defines aporia as sites of doubt or perplexity where the apparent coherence of the text can be unraveled. "They're wasting wood, you should use it as paper" qualifies, for it is a statement that seems to make sense, seems to be coherent and quite ordinary, until we work on it for a while and discover that it is an inversion of commonsense meaning that marks a site of incoherence or tension in the larger text. "Chinese eyes" is aporetic in a different way. Unlike "They're wasting wood," which on first reading seems innocuous, "Chinese eyes" is a statement that immediately strikes us as being laden with meaning. But like "wasting wood," "Chinese eyes" has an initial clarity that becomes muddled once it is subjected to textual analysis.

I've focused my interpretations of the children's talk not just on aporia, but more generally on key moments in the transcripts that I find puzzling, odd, or awry. Aporia are sites in a text that seem coherent until they are deconstructed; in contrast, most of the moments I've focused on in this book are just the opposite—seemingly incoherent statements by children that, like the psychoanalytic symptom or the clue at a crime scene, can be shown through investigation to be meaningful. One category of seemingly incoherent utterances is enthymemes, statements that seem odd or incoherent until we supply a missing but implied step in the argument. An example would be Dylan's comment that the bad guys in *Swiss Family Robinson* are the ones without horses and the good guys the ones without hats. Voloshinov (1926/ 1976a) defines an enthymeme as "a form of syllogism one of whose premises is not expressed but assumed. For example: 'Socrates is man, therefore he is mortal.' The assumed premise: 'All men are mortal'" (p. 100). Voloshinov points out that the literal Greek meaning of enthymeme as "something located in the heart or mind" is misleading, for the enthymeme is located not inside any one individual but in the discursive space shared by interlocutors. For an enthymeme to work, the speaker must count on his listeners' sharing a sense of that which can be assumed and therefore need not be said. An outsider listening in on a discussion (for instance, an adult researcher conducting focus group interviews in an elementary school) will hear statements that sound illogical but make sense to the insiders present, who readily supply the missing steps in the chain of reasoning. I've attempted to demonstrate that the identification and explication of enthymemes is an effective way to uncover key beliefs and assumptions held by a community of speakers.

Voloshinov's notion of enthymeme is a special case of what Pierre Macherey (1978) calls the *non-dit* (the unsaid). Enthymemes are left unsaid because the speaker believes that saying them is unnecessary. Other thoughts are left unsaid because they are too horrible or dangerous to say aloud or even to think about for very long. Still others are left unsaid because the speaker lacks the words or conceptual framework needed to express them. Macherey suggests that texts, like people, have an unconscious and thus there is no text "which is completely self-conscious, aware of the means of its own realisation, aware of what it is doing" (p. 27). This version of the *non-dit* is related to Louis Althusser's (1966) suggestion that texts have an unstated *central problematic* that must be inferred by *reading symptomatically*. Reading symptomatically is an interpretive strategy Althusser devised for reading Marx. Althusser suggests that the meaning of the points Marx was struggling with need to be dug out of rather than just read in Marx's texts. He argues that the core of Marx's message is something that Marx did not and could not fully comprehend because he was too close to the central problematic of his own work to be able to see or articulate it clearly:

> An ideology ... can be regarded as characterized ... by the fact that *its own problematic is not conscious of itself*. ... An ideology is ... unconscious of its "theoretical presuppositions", that is, the active but unavowed problematic which fixes for it the meaning and movement of its problems and thereby of their solutions. So a problematic generally cannot be read like an open book, it must be dragged up from the depths of the ideology in which it is buried but active. (p. 69; emphasis in original)

Althusser conceived of reading symptomatically as a strategy for uncovering the central problematic of sophisticated scholarly texts such as Marx's *Capital*. I propose that this approach can work as well as a strategy to reveal the "unavowed problematic" in transcripts of children's talk. An example of where I drag a problematic "up from the depths of the ideology in which it is buried but active" would be my analysis of Dan, Beau, Jordan, and Stacy's talk about violence in Chapter 2. The children's seemingly naive and contradictory statements can be read, following Althusser, as an insightful if not fully developed critique of the media effects debate, a critique that works to expose deep anxiety and confusion in our society involving the interrelationship of violence, imitation, representation, and masculinity.

Slovoj Zizek (1991) enjoins us to *look awry* at texts. Zizek looks awry at "things that stick out" (uncanny, odd moments in a text that beg for interpretation, such as the key clue in a Hitchcock thriller, for instance, the windmill that rotates backwards in *Foreign Correspondent*). Zizek took this idea from Jacques Lacan (1993), who searches in his patients' speech and dreams for *pointes de capiton* (quilting points), sites in a text where surface and deep levels of meaning are tied together. Aporia, enthymemes, the *non-dit*, central problematics, quilting points, things that stick out, the uncanny: in a few paragraphs, I have sketched out what can only be the beginnings of a project of sorting out a taxonomy of related terms for describing the not fully articulated but nevertheless present meanings of a text.

THE MEDIA EFFECTS DEBATE REVISITED

In the Introduction, I criticized the tendency of media researchers to analyze the television shows and movies children watch rather than talking to children about these texts. I suggested that this approach is epistemologically unsound because meaning lies not in the media text alone but in the interaction of a viewer and a text. We can see now that the problem with text-based approaches to studying children and the media is not only or primarily epistemological. Why do media researchers and other adults feel they can write confidently about the meaning of a text intended for children without talking to children? We need to explicate the unstated but implied steps of the enthymeme: researchers, teachers, and other adults can understand media effects on children solely by analyzing texts because children are naive, ignorant, and vulnerable media consumers who unthinkingly soak up the meanings of the noxious media texts to which they are exposed.

I disagree with these assumptions about the power media texts hold over children. I am not suggesting that children's readings are always insightful and resistant. Rather, my position is that we cannot know in advance of doing research how particular children will make sense of particular media texts. We've seen examples in this book of children endorsing as well as resisting ideological messages in the media. I've suggested that differences in the meanings children make of media texts are most usefully understood as reflections of differences in the local discourse communities to which they belong. When children fail to read racist, sexist, or colonialist media messages resistantly, the essence of the problem may lie not in their childish naiveté or ignorance but in something that is lacking or remiss in the community in which they live and make meaning. This is the core insight of Voloshinov's *Freudianism: A Marxist Critique* (1926/1976b). Emotional, cognitive, and moral confusion in individuals reflects the tensions, hypocrisies, and moral failings of the larger community. Similarly, instances of resistance to dominant ideological messages in the popular media are most usefully understood as reflections not of an individual's strength of character or level of cognitive development but of the individual's participation in a discourse community that includes compelling resistant voices. Where, as at Koa, children are exposed to complex discourses on race and culture, they are well positioned to offer readings of *Swiss Family Robinson* that challenge the film's racism and colonialism. Where, as at Koa, children lack exposure to critical discourses on class and heteronormativity, they have difficulty marshaling resistant readings of the film's relentless valorization of patriarchy and bourgeois family values.

Children also resist ideological hailing unintentionally, the way a block of marble resists being turned into a bust. It's not a matter of the marble having the will to resist becoming a work of art—it's just that marble is not all that malleable. So too, I suspect, is the case with children's notions of race, violence, class, and gender. For better or worse, it's not that easy to mold children's understandings of these issues. Children can watch a movie full of ideological messages we find repugnant, and emerge unscathed, just as they can go through a lesson full of educational messages we find uplifting and come out having learned little or nothing. Whether children embrace or resist a lesson or a media message is a very complex, contingent, and contextual question, a question that can be answered only by doing careful, nuanced readings of specific children's interactions with specific cultural texts. This is what I have attempted to do in this book.

LOCAL KIDS, GLOBAL CULTURE

One of the core anxieties about the media is that local communities will be homogenized by globally circulating media texts. The result will be a loss of local cultures, identities, languages, and meanings. In this scenario, the bad guys are the American movie, television, and music industries. Politicians, cultural critics, and educators in many parts of the world often use "Americanization" as a synonym for "globalization" (Mattelart, Delcourt, & Mattelart 1984; Meyrowitz, 1986). This is understandable, as the United States undeniably is the site of the production of many of the most powerful globally circulating products and messages. But I think it is a mistake to conceptualize the global and the local primarily in national terms. Hollywood is just one of several key sites (along with London, Tokyo, New York, Delhi, Sydney, Berlin, Mexico City, and São Paulo) for the production and circulation of media messages that impact far-flung local communities. Movie-making is one of the most international of industries—the production, direction, acting, and technical work on a Hollywood film are almost always a multinational effort. For example, *Swiss Family Robinson* is based on a 19th-century book by a Swiss author, which in turn was based on an 18th-century English novel. The director of the movie (Ken Annakin) is English, as is the lead actor, John Mills. The villain is played by a Japanese actor. The movie is set on an island in the Indian Ocean but was filmed on the Caribbean island of Tobago. The movie is full of ideological messages that people in many communities would no doubt find objectionable. But these ideological messages are not necessarily any more American than they are British or Swiss. What I am suggesting is that if we are to understand the impact of cultural texts produced in metropolitan centers on local communities, it is necessary to get beyond a 19th-century preoccupation with nations and think instead in terms of a worldwide circulation of messages that flow between core cultural and economic zones and less powerful (but not powerless) peripheral regions. Hollywood is both bigger and smaller than the United States—bigger in that it draws on capital, labor, and ideas from around the globe; smaller in the sense that it doesn't always (or ever) speak for the rest of the country. The ideological messages coming out of Hollywood most often have American accents, but the representation of race, class, and gender in Hollywood movies raises concerns that transcend national boundaries.

In Hawai'i, people who speak pidgin, eat *plate lunch,* listen to *Jawaiian* (Hawaiian reggae) music, and prefer rubber slippers to any other footwear refer to themselves as *locals.* The children at Koa Elementary School are local not just in this Hawaiian meaning of the term but also in the way that children everywhere are local. Like children in a village in Mexico, an inner-city neighborhood in Liverpool, or a suburb of Osaka, the children at Koa are local because most of their days are spent within a few square miles, or even square blocks, where they deal with a relatively small number of adults (parents, neighbors, teachers, storekeepers). It is within such local settings that children make sense of media.

Children draw on their local experiences, discourses, and knowledge to make sense of the global culture that comes to them not only through books, but, more importantly these days, through television, movies, music, video games, and the Internet. The global media culture, as cultural critics point out, is powerful and potentially homogenizing. But this global culture is consumed and given meaning locally, where globally circulating texts interact with local discourses (Hall, 1991/1997). As David Morley (1980) writes,

> The meaning of the text will be constructed differently according to the discourses (knowledges, prejudices, resistances, etc.) brought to bear on the text by the reader and the crucial factor in the encounter of audience/subject and text will be the range of discourses at the disposal of the audience. (p. 18)

In just this way, the representation of race in *Swiss Family Robinson* is understood by the children at Koa in the context of the discourses on race that circulate in the local community. Race and ethnicity are being negotiated daily in Hawai'i in ways that challenge Hollywood versions. My point is not that race is an unproblematic category in Hawai'i, but that the fluidity of race relations in Hawai'i and the presence of multiple discourses on race mean that the children at Koa bring valuable prior knowledge to their understanding of the depiction of race relations in *Swiss Family Robinson*. We have seen the children at Koa make sense of *Swiss Family Robinson* by reading this text alongside their previous experiences and alongside other texts they have been exposed to that speak meaningfully to them about race. Some of these texts originate outside Hawai'i (for instance, chapters in their textbooks that discuss the discovery and settlement of the United States). Some are local and authoritative (for example, their fourth-grade curriculum in Hawaiian studies). Some are local and subversive (for example, the routines of local comedians who do parodies of Hawaii's ethnic groups, which the children at Koa find scandalous, hilarious, and familiar). Other discourses on race are local in a micrological sense, as they reflect specific features and tensions of life at Koa School. For instance, at the time of our interviews, a game played at Koa during recess, when the children from the two schools-within-a-school came together, was called Hawaiians and Haoles. The game was played like Cowboys and Indians, with the "Hawaiians" being the kids from the Hawaiian-language immersion program and the *"haoles"* the kids from the other two programs, only a handful of whom were Caucasian.

Most studies of media effects on children have failed to take account of the local contexts and of the fact that meanings, even of globally circulating media products, are made locally. Thus a question such as "Are children hurt by the racism of *Swiss Family Robinson?*" is unanswerable because it doesn't specify which children we are talking about. We cannot know from analyzing the contents of a movie what it will mean to a particular group of children. Without doing careful, contextualized research, we cannot know, for instance, what effect representations in a film of stereotypical Oriental villains will have on Japanese American children living in various localities. Media representations of race will be experienced differently by Japanese American children living in different local contexts—for instance, in Peoria, Illinois, where there are only a handful of Japanese Americans, and in Pearl City, Hawai'i, where, at the time of this study, the senators from Hawai'i were Japanese American, as were most of Koa's teachers.

The contextuality of media meanings has been a central thesis of this book: potentially noxious media messages have pernicious effects differentially, and these differences reflect the unique character of the local communities in which media texts are consumed and given meaning. A key factor in the meanings children make of an ideological message in a media text is the presence or absence in their local community of counterdiscourses. Local communities, such as a school, are sites where discordant voices and opinions meet, clash, and interact. Even within one small local setting, we have found a diversity of life experience leading to a diversity in the children's ability to marshal resistant readings of media texts. Michael, who recently moved to Pearl City from a town on the U.S. mainland, found nothing wrong with the race relations and colonial politics of *Swiss Family Robinson*. In contrast, Clem, one of the few African American students in the school, introduced trenchant points about race and power, and Punihei, the daughter of a Hawaiian studies professor and sovereignty activist, offered a politically informed critique of the film. Each of the students at Koa brought a unique combination of experiences, interests, and intertextual associations to the discussions of *Swiss Family Robinson*. As a result, these discussions are wonderfully heterogeneous social texts that reward our efforts at close reading and imaginative interpretation.

References

Abercrombie, N., Hill, S. & Turner, B. (1980). *The dominant ideology thesis.* London: Allen & Unwin.

Althusser, L. (1966). *For Marx.* London: Penguin Books.

Althusser, L. (1972). *Lenin and philosophy, and other essays* (B. Brewster, trans.). New York: Monthly Review Press.

Ang, I. (1985). *Watching* Dallas: *Soap opera and the melodramatic imagination.* London: Methuen.

Bakhtin, M. (1981). Discourse in the novel (M. Holquist & C. Emerson, Trans.). In M. Holquist (Ed.), *Dialogic imagination: Four essays.* (pp. 259–422). Austin: University of Texas Press.

Bakhtin, M. (1986). *Speech genres and other late essays* (V. McGee, Trans.). Austin: University of Texas Press.

Bakhtin, M. (1990). *Art and answerability* (M. Holquist & V. Liapunov, Trans.). Austin: University of Texas Press.

Barker, M. (1989). *Comics: Ideology, power and the critics.* Manchester: Manchester University Press.

Barker, M. (1997). *Ill effects: The media/violence debate.* London: Routledge.

Bell, E., Haas, L., & Sells, L. (1995). *From mouse to mermaid: The politics of film, gender, and culture.* Bloomington: Indiana University Press.

Bettelheim, B. (1972). *The empty fortress.* New York: Free Press.

Boldt, G. (1997). Sexist and heterosexist responses to gender bending. In J. Tobin (Ed.), *Making a place for pleasure in early childhood education.* (pp. 188–213). New Haven: Yale University Press.

Briggs, J. (1998). *Inuit morality play: The emotional education of a three-year-old.* New Haven: Yale University Press.

Buckingham, D. (1993). *Children talking television.* London: Falmer.

Buckingham, D. (1996). *Moving images: Understanding children's emotional responses to television.* Manchester: Manchester University Press.

Butler, J. (1990). *Gender trouble.* New York: Routledge.

Butler, J. (1993). *Bodies that matter.* New York: Routledge.

Cazden, C. (1987). *Classroom discourse: The language of teaching and learning.* Portsmouth, NH: Heinemann.

Clark, C. (1995). *Flights of fancy, leaps of faith: Children's myths in contemporary America.* Chicago: University of Chicago Press.

Clark, K., & Holquist, M. (1984). *Mikhail Bakhtin.* Cambridge, MA: Harvard University Press.

Clover, C. (1992). *Men, women, and chainsaws: Gender in the modern horror film.* Princeton, NJ: Princeton University Press.

de Certeau, M. (1984). *The practice of everyday life.* Berkeley: University of California Press.

Dentith, S. (1995). *Bakhtinian thought: An introductory reader.* London: Routledge.

Derrida, J. (1976). *Of grammatology* (G. Spivak, Trans.). Baltimore and London: Johns Hopkins University Press.

Derrida, J. (1992). Structure, sign and play in the discourse of the human sciences. In P. Rice & P. Waugh (Eds.), *Modern literary theory: A reader.* (pp. 149–165). London: Arnold.

Dorfman, A. (1983). *The empire's old clothes: What the Lone Ranger, Babar, and other innocent heroes do to our minds.* New York: Penguin.

Dorfman, A., & Mattelart, A. (1984). *How to read Donald Duck: Imperialist ideology in the Disney comic.* New York: International General Editions.

Douglas, M. (1966). *Purity and danger: an analysis of concepts of pollution and taboo.* London: Routledge & Kegan Paul.

Dyson, A. H. (1997). *Writing superheroes.* New York: Teachers College Press.

Engelhardt, T. (1987). Ambush at kamikaze pass. In D. Lazere (Ed.), *American media and mass culture.* (pp. 480–498). Berkeley: University of California Press.

Erikson, E. (1964). *Childhood and society.* New York: W. W. Norton.

Fanon, F. (1963). *The wretched of the earth.* New York: Grove.

Fish, S. (1982). *Is there a text in this class?* Cambridge: Harvard University Press.

Fiske, J. (1987). *Television culture.* New York: Routledge.

Fiske, J. (1989). *Reading the popular.* Boston: Unwin Hyman.

Freud, S. (1974). *The psychopathology of everyday life.* In J. Strachey (Ed. and Trans.). *The standard edition of the complete psychological works of Sigmund Freud* (Vol. 6). London: Hogarth. (Original work published 1901)

Foucault, M. (1979). *Discipline and punish.* (A. Sheridan, Trans.). New York: Vintage.

Gerbner, G. (1970). Cultural indicators: The case of violence in television drama. *Annals of the American Association of Political and Social Science, 338,* 69–81.

Gillespie, M. (1995). *Television, ethnicity, and cultural change.* London: Routledge.

Gilman, S. (1991). *The Jew's body.* New York: Routledge.

Giroux, H. (1997). Are Disney movies good for your kids? In S. Steinberg & J. Kincheloe (Eds.), *Kinderculture: The corporate construction of childhood.* (pp. 53–68). Boulder, CO: Westview.

Grace, D. & Tobin, J. (1997). Carnival in the classroom: Elementary students making videos. In J. Tobin (Ed.), *Making a place for pleasure in early childhood education.* (pp. 159–187). New Haven: Yale University Press.

Hall, S. (1991/1997). The local and the global: Globalization and ethnicity. In A. King (Ed.), *Culture, globalization and the world-system: Contemporary conditions for the representation of identity.* (pp. 19–40). Minneapolis: University of Minnesota Press.

Hall, S. (1999). Encoding, decoding. In S. During (Ed.), *The cultural studies reader.* (pp. 507–517). London: Routledge.

Hobson, D. (1982). Crossroads: *The drama of a soap opera.* London: Methuen.

Hodge, B., & Tripp, D. (1986). *Children and television: A semiotic approach.* Cambridge: Polity.

Iser, W. (1974). *The implied reader.* Baltimore: Johns Hopkins University Press.

Jhally, S., & Lewis, J. (1992). *Enlighted racism:* The Cosby Show *audiences, and the myth of the American dream.* Boulder, CO: Westview.

Kame'eleihiwa, L. (1992). *Native land and foreign desires.* Honolulu: Bishop Museum Press.

Kono, J. (1995). *Tsunami years.* Honolulu: Bamboo Ridge Press.

Lacan, J. (1993). *The seminar: Book III, the psychoses, 1955–56.* (R. Grigg, Trans.). London: Routledge.

Leavitt, R. L. (1994). *Power and emotion in infant-toddler daycare.* State University of New York Press, Albany.

Lévi-Strauss, C. (1969). *The raw and the cooked* (J. and D. Weightman, Trans.). New York: Harper & Row.

Liebes, T., & Katz, E. (1990). *The export of meaning: Cross-cultural readings of* Dallas. New York: Oxford University Press.

Losing his head. (1997, September 15). *Sports Illustrated.* pp. 48–55.

McLaren, P., & Morris, J. (1997). *Mighty Morphin Power Rangers: The aesthetics of phallo-militaristic justice.* In S. Steinberg & J. Kincheloe (Eds.), *Kinderculture.* (pp. 115–128). Boulder, CO: Westview.

Macherey, P. (1978). *A theory of literary production* (G. Wall, Trans.). London: Routledge & Kegan Paul.

Mattelart, A., Delcourt, X., & Mattelart, M. (1984). *International image markets: In search of an alternative perspective.* London: Allen & Unwin.

Meyrowitz, J. (1986). *No sense of place: The impact of electronic media on social behavior.* New York: Oxford University Press.

Miller, P. (1982). *Wendy, Amy, and Beth: Learning language in South Baltimore.* Austin: University of Texas Press.

Miller, P., Hoogstra, L., Mintz, J., Fung, H., & Williams, K. (1993). Troubles in the garden and how they get resolved: A young child's transformation of his favorite story. In C. Nelson (Ed.), *Memory and affect in development: The Minnesota Symposia on Child Psychology 26,* 87–113. Hillsdale, NJ: Erlbaum.

Morley, D. (1980). *The nationwide audience: Structure and decoding.* London: British Film Institute.

Morley, D. (1986). *Family television: Cultural power and domestic leisure.* London: Routledge.

Mulvey, L. (1975). Visual pleasure and narrative cinema. *Screen, 16*(3), 6–18.

Newkirk, T. (1988). *More than stories: The range of children's writing.* Portsmouth, NH: Heinemann.

Newkirk, T. (1992). *Listening in: Children talk about books (and other things).* Portsmouth, NH: Heinemann.

Nightingale, V. (1996). *Studying audiences: The shock of the real.* New York: Routledge.

Ohta, R., & Tobin, J. (1995). Video literacy at Waiau School. *Kamehameha Journal of Education, 6,* 91–104.

Paley, V. (1981). *Wally's stories: Conversations in the kindergarten.* Cambridge, MA: Harvard University Press.

Paley, V. (1984). *Boys and girls: Superheroes in the doll corner.* Chicago: University of Chicago Press.

Paley, V. (1991). *Bad guys don't have birthdays: Fantasy play at four.* Chicago: University of Chicago Press.

Phelan, P. (1993). *The unmarked: The politics of performance.* New York: Routlege.

Project on Disney, The. (1995). *Inside the mouse: Work and play at Disney World.* Durham, NC: Duke University Press.

Provenzo, E. (1991). *Video kids: Making sense of Nintendo.* Cambridge, MA: Harvard University Press.

Radway, J. (1984). *Reading the romance: Women, patriarchy, and popular literature.* Chapel Hill: University of North Carolina Press.

Sadker, M., & Sadker, D. (1995). *Failing at fairness: How our schools cheat girls.* New York: Touchstone Books.

Said, E. (1979). *Orientalism.* New York: Vintage.

Sarup, M. (1993). *An introductory guide to post-structuralism and postmodernism.* Athens: University of Georgia Press.

Saussure, F. (1959). *Course in general linguistics.* New York: Philosophical library.

Sefton-Green, J. (1990). Culture and *The Cosby Show.* In D. Buckingham & J. Sefton-Green (Eds.), *Watching Media Learning.* (pp. 127–150). London: Falmer.

Sefton-Green, J. (1993). Untidy, depressing, and violent: A boy's own story. In D. Buckingham (Ed.), *Reading audiences: Young people and the media.* (pp. 135–158). Manchester: Manchester University Press.

Shohat, E., & Stam, R. (1994). *Unthinking eurocentrism: Multiculturalism and the media.* New York: Routledge.

Slaughter, H. (1997). Indigenous language immersion in Hawai'i: A case study of Kula Kaiapuni Hawai'i, an effort to save the indigenous language of Hawai'i. In R. Johnson & M. Swain (Eds.), *Immersion education: International perspectives.* (pp. 105–130). Cambridge: Cambridge University Press.

Smoodin, E. (1994). *Disney discourse: Producing the Magic Kingdom.* New York: Routledge.

Tamura, E. (1994). *Americanization, acculturation, and ethnic identity: The Nisei generation in Hawaii.* Honolulu: University of Hawaii Press.

Thorne, B. (1993). *Gender play: Girls and boys in school.* Newark, NJ: Rutgers University Press.

Tobias, S. (1990). *They're not dumb, they're different: Stalking the second tier.* Tuscon: Research Corporation.

Tobin, J. (1997). *Making a place for pleasure in early childhood education.* New Haven: Yale University Press.

Tobin, J., Wu, D., & Davidson, D. (1989). *Preschool in three cultures: Japan, China, and the United States.* New Haven: Yale University Press.

Todorov, T. (1984). *Mikhail Bakhtin: The dialogical principle.* Minneapolis: University of Minnesota Press.

Tompkins, J. (1980). *Reader-response criticism.* Baltimore: Johns Hopkins University Press.

Voloshinov, V. (1976a). Discourse in life and discourse in art. In N. Bruss (Ed.), *Freudianism: A Marxist critique* (I. R. Titunik, Trans.). New York: Academic Press. (Original work published in 1926)

Voloshinov, V. (1976b). *Freudianism: A Marxist critique* (N. Bruss, Ed.; I. R. Titunik, Trans.). New York: Academic Press. (Original work published in 1927)

Walkerdine, V. (1990). Sex, power, and pedagogy. In *Schoolgirl fictions*. London: Verso.

Yamanaka, L. (1993). *Saturday night at the Pahala Theatre*. Honolulu: Bamboo Ridge Press.

Yamanaka, L. (1996). *Wild meat and the bully burgers*. New York: Farrar, Straus & Giroux.

Yamauchi, L., Ceppi, A., & Lau-Smith, J. (1999). Sociocultural influences on the development of Papahana Kaiapuni, the Hawaiian language immersion program. *Journal of Education for Students Placed at Risk, 4,* 27–46.

Zizek, S. (1991). *Looking awry: An introduction to Jacques Lacan through popular culture*. Cambridge: M.I.T. Press.

Index

About the Author

Joseph Tobin is a professor in the Department of Teacher Education and Curriculum Studies at the University of Hawai'i, Manoa, where he works with preservice and in-service teachers in a Hawaiian-language immersion program, teaches qualitative research methods, and advises graduate students. Among his publications are *Preschool in Three Cultures*, *Remade in Japan*, and *Making a Place for Pleasure in Early Childhood Education*.